THE COMPLETE BOOK OF
MOTORCYCLES

Motorcycling means many different things to many different people. On the previous page, N. Mackenzie accelerates his enormously powerful Yamaha through a bend. On this page, a classic Harley-Davidson FXRS awaits the return of its rider on a forest path. Overleaf, howling and whining, dirt bikes compete in a pack in the Winston Supercross.

Designed by Sally Strugnell
Edited by David Gibbon

2904
This edition published in 1994 by
   Tiger Books International PLC, London
© 1993 CLB Publishing Ltd,
   Godalming, Surrey
Printed and bound in Spain
   by Graficromo, S.A.
ISBN 1-85501-396-7

THE COMPLETE BOOK OF
MOTORCYCLES

Roger W. Hicks

TIGER BOOKS INTERNATIONAL
LONDON

CONTENTS

DREAMS & MEMORIES

The smell of cooking fires in a hot, dusty landscape; the steady bomp … bomp … bomp of a big single, loud enough to be music, quiet enough not to shatter the spell. The road becomes a two-rutter, a one-rutter, a footpath, peters out. You continue across the dry earth of what will, when the rainy season returns, once again be a rice-paddy. Somewhere ahead there is an old temple. You want to see it. – Motorcycle touring in India.

The howl of a super-tuned two-stroke: the razor's edge of concentration as you look for a gap, see it, squeeze through. A momentary awareness of the rich smells of burnt oil and hot rubber, of the sun pouring down like honey on a Sunday afternoon, then it's the next corner. Select the line, flicking down through the six-speed box, braking, holding the speed on the curve, accelerating onto the next straight. – Racing.

Clogged traffic, again. Ten miles an hour, five miles an hour, stop. You split the lanes: not too fast, but at least you are moving. Some of the drivers, trapped in their cages, smile and give you the thumbs-up. Others are visibly angry that you are not trapped like them. You smile at both kinds. The mountains or the beach, you can be there before they can. – The week-end.

A plume of soft earth rooster-tails from the rear wheel as you land, the long-travel soft suspension soaking up the shocks. The back end slides momentarily; you correct it with the broad bars, rising again on the footrests as you shift your weight to balance the machine. Mud from the stream-bed at the bottom of the hill cakes your boots. You laugh from sheer exhilaration. – Dirt.

Idly, you fantasize. If you could have any bike here, which would it be? The SS80? No, if you wanted a Brough, you'd do it properly: an SS100, a Pendine. The Vinnie, then, maybe, its huge black crank-cases the ultimate fantasy engine. Or there's the

Even more than a four-wheel-drive, a motorcycle has the potential to be a "go-anywhere" vehicle (left) for exploring back roads, dirt paths and even places where there are no tracks at all. Or, of course, it can be almost completely divorced from function, like the Triumph chop (above).

INTRODUCTION

LEFT: *A non-motorcyclist would never understand: there has never been a make of motorcycle called a Triton. But the recipe is simple. You take a powerful Triumph engine out of its less-than-impressive frame, and put it into a sweet-handling Norton frame from which you have removed a less-than-powerful motor. The result is the definitive British classic twin; and you call it a Triton because Norumph would be silly. The simplicity and modular design of older motorcycles made such engine swaps easy: there are even Norvins, Vincent engines in Norton frames. The Norton "featherbed" is probably the greatest frame of all time.*

Harley in full California Highway Patrol rig, except that the spec. card says there's a hundred-inch engine and all the Screaming Eagle good stuff. But it looks gross next to the petite elegance of the 1948 Speed Twin – and if you wanted gross, of course, there's the turbo Kwacker 1300 with the purple metalflake paint and the murals and the gold-plated brightwork. Hell, that thing must be good for a hundred and fifty, easy. If you could stay on it. – The motorcycle show.

A sudden burst of laughter from the table in the corner makes you look up. New people; certainly, you've never seen her before, the one with the long blonde hair and the slightly-too-new black leather jacket, the one who looks like something out of a motorcycle ad. Another rider comes in, drops his helmet (carefully!) on the pile beside the door, walks over to her table. She hugs him. You take another pull on your beer. – Saturday night at the Mardyke Arms.

Creaming down the Interstate, the off-beat rumble of the eighty-inch Evo all but drowned by the music on the stereo. You're actually inside the speed limit, but hey, who cares? The lady on the back strokes the shoulder of your leathers; she's enjoying it too. You glance at your watch. You should be in Jamestown by six; dinner at the National hotel, a room with a bath, a long soak to ease the muscles, then early to bed. – California dreamin'.

Rain coming down in sheets, and you're fifteen miles from nowhere. You've checked the fuel lines, the high-tension and low-tension connections, the spark itself. You have offered up prayers to Vulcan, Hephaestus, Thor, all the gods who might have something to do with heathen motorcycles. This time, it's got to start, or it's hitch-hiking time. Gingerly, almost tentatively, you find compression and swing on the kick-start. With a bang and a splutter, the Commando starts up. Suddenly, the last forty-five minutes of cold and misery and desperation are forgotten. You're on the road again.

Somewhere in that melange of dreams and memories there must be something that strikes a chord. Not the same experience, maybe, but one that's close enough. Motorcycles are more than transport, more than speed and acceleration, more than freedom

itself. They are the embodiment of the old Arab proverb: *Take what you want, and pay for it, sayeth the Lord.* There's another saying, too, from the 1960s: *Not all highs are good highs.* You remember this when you are standing at the side of the road, shaking. The gearshift linkage snapped, and you went around the corner in fifth instead of fourth, ten to fifteen miles an hour faster than you intended, and there's bright metal where you grounded the foot-rests, the centre-stand and even the exhaust pipes. The sole of your left boot is visibly chamfered on the outside by a quarter of an inch. And yet you did it. You dragged the old girl around the corner on the ragged edge, six inches from the gravel that would have had you into the crash barrier at eighty miles an hour. Slowly, as the terror ebbs away, a sneaky little seed begins to sprout. That wasn't so bad after all. It's a part of what riding a bike is about. You pat the motorcycle on the tank. "Hey," you say, "We did it!" Maybe all highs *are* good highs.

Anyone who buys a motorcycle is buying a dream. Well, *almost* anybody. It's true that there are some people who buy two-wheelers just for transport. There are the broken-down men in grubby ex-War Department mackintoshes who ride rusty old mopeds from which every vestige of everything has long ago vanished, the barest, bleakest form of two-wheeled powered transport you can find, whose resale value is probably less than that of a respectable twelve-speed mountain bike. There are cabbies-in-waiting, wobbling around London with their clip-boards of street-names and road-maps, getting the Knowledge that will get them their Hackney Carriage tickets. There are those incredibly decrepit CX500s which no-one ever seems to ride, but which must move because they are there all day and then gone in the evening. But who knows? Maybe even those CX500s belong to people who are secretly restoring Black Lightnings, or racing FZ750s at weekends, and who just wanted a totally reliable, ride-it-and-forget-it hack for everyday use. And in most of Europe, of course, everyone uses mopeds as cheap transport: you see grandmothers coming home from the market, children on the way to school, comic-book Frenchmen with berets on their heads and a baguette on the luggage carrier, trailing clouds of Gauloise smoke and two-stroke oil.

ABOVE: *There are some motorcycles where everything is so right, so very nearly perfect, that no-one but a madman or a barbarian (or possibly a racer) would* *want to modify them. The immortal Brough Superior SS100 is such a machine. Immensely powerful – each SS100 was guaranteed in writing to have exceeded 100* *mph as early as the 1920s – they were also superbly styled and beautifully finished. Often called "the Rolls-Royce of motorcycles," legend has it that Rolls-* *Royce did not dispute the appellation. Even today, riding a Brough is one of life's great motorcycling experiences.*

INTRODUCTION

RIGHT: *You can almost smell the mud and feel the sting of the water on your cheeks in this superb picture of the Swiss rider Anton Durre at the International Six Days Event (I.S.D.E.) in 1983. The I.S.D.E., formerly the I.S.D.T. ("Trials" rather than "Event") is to off-road riding what Grand Prix racing is to fast road riding: the same thing, but carried to a degree and a pitch of concentration which most people cannot even imagine, let alone hope to emulate.*

Riding fast across rough terrain is one of the greatest thrills on two wheels; but it is also one of the most dangerous, and one which requires first-class preparation of both bike and rider. When you plough through a stretch of water already muddied by previous riders, you do not even know how deep it is, and you do not know what is under your wheels: rock, mud, sand or even weed.

That fine exhilaration as the water flies up in a cloud of spray is tempered by the realization that you can always fall off – and if you do, it will probably hurt, despite modern "body armour" protective clothing.

The motorcycle is far more evolved than those old "scramblers," too. Huge knobbly tyres grip the most appalling surfaces with conviction, while brakes and electrics have to be designed to withstand onslaughts of water and mud which would stop any ordinary machine.

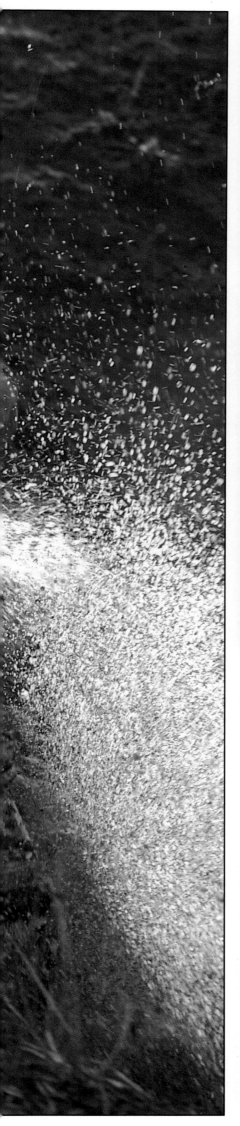

Generally, though, there is a common bond between the sixteen-year-old on his moped tricked out to look like a racer; the yuppie on his Laverda or Ducati Paso; the woman in her thirties on the Moto-Guzzi V50; the "one percenter" on his Harley; and the greybeard riding sedately (but surprisingly quickly) on his BMW Boxer. For their various reasons, they have all made a conscious decision to stand out from the crowd.

The bond between motorcyclists is something that is easier to experience than to describe, though, and a lot of it comes down to shared experience. In return for the kind of acceleration that is only available from a handful of staggeringly-expensive motor cars, the motorcyclist accepts a complex, highly-stressed machine which has to be kept in good mechanical order and which occasionally (or in some cases, often) falls from mechanical grace.

In return for the kind of go-anywhere ability that is normally associated only with pedestrians and horse-riders, the motorcyclist accepts a tremendous vulnerability to other road-users, and a responsibility for his or her own errors of judgement. If you run out of road, you are almost certain to fall off – and the only "crumple zone" on a motorcycle is *you*.

In return for a seemingly unmediated communion with reality, where warm sun becomes an almost liquid cold in the shadow of trees and the air you breathe is always the air of this moment with its freight of scents and stenches, clarity or dust, the motorcyclist accepts an enormous vulnerability to the elements; the wind, rain and snow. You can't wind up the windows on a motorcycle.

ABOVE: *A skilled dirt-bike rider can persuade his machine to climb over obstacles which anyone can plainly see are insurmountable: this is Britain's Adam Norris on a particularly tricky slope. This constant struggle for mastery of both machine and terrain is one of the great attractions of any type of motorcycling. The thing is that you are always pitted against yourself: a truly skilled rider can work miracles with an inferior machine, but a poor rider will fall off even the finest motorcycle he can buy. The combination of a good rider and a good machine, as seen here, can have an almost balletic grace.*

ABOVE: *It is perfectly possible to combine different areas of interest in motorcycling: for instance, competitive dirt riding on old motorcycles, like Jason Peeling's 1964 Greeves 250. Road racing on vintage motorcycles is another possibility: a Goldie or a Thruxton sounds and looks just as good today as it did when it was a state-of-the-art racer. Other riders may take apparently unsuitable roadsters off road: it is amazing where even a fully-laden BMW R100RS can go.*

RIGHT: *Many motorcyclists reckon that motorcycling is like sex: the next best thing to doing it is talking about it. A ride to the Ace Cafe, or a friendly pub, provides an excuse for a ride and a place to talk when you arrive.*

FACING PAGE: *Camping and motorcycling seem to go naturally together: a cynic might say that with both you spend a good deal of the time cold, wet and uncomfortable. Admittedly, there are times when it is like this and when you wonder why on earth you do it. But when it goes right – ah, no-one could fault it. An attractive campsite; good weather; the company of like-minded friends; and a long, liquid evening, after which you stagger into your tent to sleep off the day's excesses. In the United States there are rallies which are centered on hotels, but in most of the rest of the world, it's camping time. This is at the 1989 T.T. races, when more conventional accommodation is all but impossible to come by anyway.*

And yet, despite this bond, motorcyclists are also a fractious, factitious bunch. Harley and Triumph riders look down on "Jap crap." Heavy-duty tourers on their Goldwings and Ventures look down on the "crotch rocket" roadburners. If you don't ride a BMW boxer, the German twins are antiques, living fossils; if you don't ride a Harley-Davidson, the big American bikes are dinosaurs and they vibrate like cement mixers. A Goldwing, to the sporting rider, is a Leadwing. Italian bikes are the *ne plus ultra* of motorcycling, and anyone who rides anything else is a fool who doesn't know what handling is; or alternatively, Italian bikes are rust-prone, unreliable anachronisms that can be seen off by any modern Japanese sports bike. And, of course, there are plenty of people who believe that the last "real" motorcycle was a Norton Commando, or a Vincent Series C, or a "Cammy" Norton, or a Brough Superior .... The bikes of yesteryear, now that direct comparisons with their counterparts are increasingly difficult (who would thrash a sixty-year-old motorcycle?), attract supporters and detractors who are more vociferous than they were when the bikes were in production. Try telling an *aficionado* of Indians that Harleys are any good!

And then the perspective shifts again. Motorcyclists are just like a family. Like any family, they have their high-flyers and their good-for-nothings. Like most families, there are bitter quarrels – the equivalent of the aunt that no-one has spoken to for years, the cousin who ran off to Australia. But if an outsider starts to criticize the family, suddenly they find that they have taken on more than they have bargained for. Unwashed man-mountains stand shoulder to shoulder with lawyers, grandmothers and schoolteachers. Letters pour in, laboriously scribbled on ragged sheets torn from cheap, lined notepads or elegantly word-processed on headed paper. A surprising expertise at putting a "spin" on the media

becomes apparent. And ingenious legal arguments suddenly appear: it turns out that among the ranks of motorcyclists there are constitutional lawyers, experts on the common law, students of the statutes.

Of course, the motorcyclists don't always win. Most motorcyclists, for example, support the slogan "Helmets yes, compulsion no," but every year there are fewer places where the motorcyclist is allowed to choose for himself or herself. But the more cretinous suggestions are swiftly batted down, as in the story of the California congressman who wanted motorcycles to have seat belts. The idea was scotched when one enterprising motorcyclist fitted a motorcycle with a seat belt, took it to Sacramento, and invited the congressman to try it, flattering him with a tale of what a brilliant idea it was. Then, when the congressman was safely strapped in, with the motorcycle on its centre-stand, the motorcyclist simply kicked the bike over on its side. The idea of safety belts was dropped, then and there ....

This is a book for all motorcyclists; as this chapter describes itself, a book of dreams and memories. It is dedicated to everyone who ever commuted to work on a motorcycle, or dreamed of riding in the Paris-Dakar, or admired a classic or went touring. It is dedicated to the sixteen-year-olds and the sixty-year-olds (and older, and younger), to the men and women, to the sports riders and the sedate tourists. It is dedicated to everyone whose parents told them that bikes are too dangerous today, then went misty-eyed as they recalled their own days on two wheels. It is dedicated to the people who no longer ride, and to those who still look forward to their first ride. It is dedicated to my brothers and sisters in the family of motorcycling, even the ones who ride FS1Es with the baffles taken out of the exhaust. It is dedicated to *you*.

ABOVE: *Few things are more moving than when a motorcyclist's brothers ride in cavalcade to pay tribute: this is the funeral of an Angel in Holland. Individually, the powerful engines seem to sob as they are ridden at low speeds, but the overall effect is one of rolling thunder, as though the hammer of Thor himself were smiting the ground in remembrance. Flowers contrast with dark leather and faded denim, the evanescence of the blossoms against the enduring steel of the machines; and strong men weep. The sombreness of the occasion is increased by the riders' awareness of their own mortality: they know that they are often riding a thin line between Heaven and Hell.*

FACING PAGE BOTTOM: *The Henderson straight-four is quite eclipsed by these movie posters. In the United States in particular, the "rebel" or "outlaw" image is well beloved by non-motorcyclists, who often tend to see "bikers" as potential thieves,* murderers and rapists; and women on motorcycles are clearly even more shocking. American riders are frequently astonished to learn that European motorcyclists are treated like human beings.

ABOVE: *Bike Week at Daytona Beach, Florida, attracts the good, the bad and the ugly; you will have to decide for yourself which category you allot to those who pull wheelies on Harleys. "Wheelies" are primarily an American invention:* traditionally, European riders preferred riding quickly on winding roads to low-speed stunts such as this. Until recently it was regarded as a mark of incompetence to lift the front wheel off the ground.

1
NOSTALGIA

Nostalgia, as we all know, isn't what it used to be. Gone are the days when middle-aged men could grow misty-eyed over the Brough Superiors, Vincent-HRDs, Velocette MACs, Indian Scouts, Norton Inters and Rudge Ulsters of their youth. Anyone who rode those things when they were new – or even when they were only slightly second-hand – is now rapidly leaving even middle-age behind. You are long in the tooth today if you learned to ride in the 1960s, when you might still have aspired to a Norton Commando, a Velocette Venom or Thruxton, a BSA Gold Star or an Enfield Constellation.

And yet we now have an extraordinary new phenomenon: motorcyclists who are nostalgic for motorcycles that ceased production even before they were born. We have motorcycles dragged back into production that their manufactures had thought obsolete, such as the big BMW "Boxers" which refuse to die. We have pseudo-classic motorcycles, like Honda's 500cc TT single, which is an obvious (and not very clever) homage to the Venoms and Goldies of yesteryear. And we have The Enfield India selling 1950s-style Bullet singles world-wide, including Japan. This is quite apart from the thriving market in *genuine* old motorcycles: a Vincent Black Prince from the early 1950s fetches more than the latest race-replica sports bikes.

What lies behind this nostalgia? Why does anyone want to ride motorcycles which are essentially outmoded, and which can be seen off (at least in a straight line) by modern machines of half the displacement and often of at least twice the reliability?

There are many answers. One, without a doubt, is that there are now many respectable and sober citizens in their forties, fifties and sixties who were star-struck with motorcycles as children. They can probably remember cutting up a favourite uncle's old motorcycle magazines, and that magical odour of oil and hot metal that surrounded their demi-god when he came back from a ride and flipped up his Mark goggles on his compressed-cork Everoak helmet. And while the uncle may have ridden something

Variously known as the Contraceptive and the Constipation, the Royal Enfield Constellation (the model on the left dates from 1959) was one of the fastest bikes on the road in its day; and the Brough Superior SS100 (the one above dates from 1939) was the definitive "superbike" of the 1920s and 1930s.

RIGHT: *The Henderson Ace was one of the finest of the all-American in-line fours. The 1301cc longitudinally mounted engine was laughably low-powered by modern standards, and the rear cylinders would soon overheat if it was pushed hard; but for flexibility it was unequalled, as it could be ridden in top gear at anything from a walking pace to speeds well in excess of a mile a minute. On appalling pre-war American roads, it could sustain speeds as high as the road would permit, day after day, with perfect reliability. Also, for a large-capacity four the Henderson was very light, with a small frontal area.*

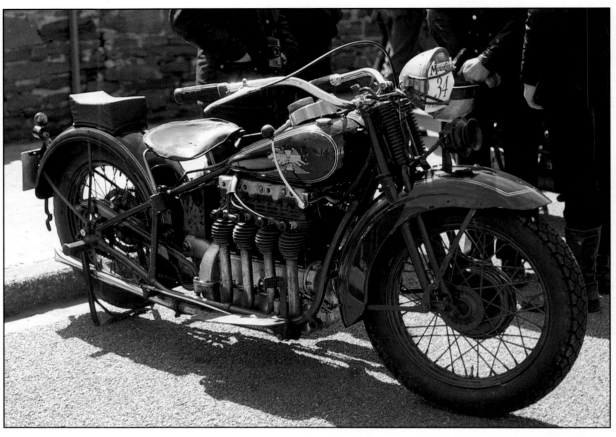

ABOVE: *This 1923 Ace is very much of its period: very long tiller-style handlebars (here dropped for a racing crouch), a flat tank, footboards, and no front brake. Note the car-type clutch, the single carburettor on an enormously long inlet tract, and the all-but-open exhaust which is actually much quieter than you might expect.*

very ordinary, such as an A65 or a Panther outfit, the bike he dreamed of was a Vincent, or a Goldie, or one of the other ultimates of a bygone age; and they inherited his dreams. Enough of these hero-worshipping six-year-olds have grown up and made enough money to buy the bikes of their childhood dreams, thereby forcing the price of the immortal motorcycles into the stratosphere.

Another reason, equally certainly, is that most motorcyclists carry around in their heads an image of what a motorcycle is supposed to look like, and of how it is supposed to work.

To begin with, you have to be able to see daylight through it: "Never trust a motorcycle you can't see through" is an article of faith with the true vintage-bike *aficionado*. A classic motorcycle wears its heart on its sleeve; or at least, it wears all its parts on its frame, which is much the same thing. You can see that if you undo *this* bolt, the foot-rest will come off; if you slack off *these* clamps, the handlebar will be freed; if you disconnect *this* cable, you won't have any brakes any more. In order to adjust the push-rods, you spin *this* nut and remove *that* cover. By taking thought, you can work out what every part does.

Also, there are certain features as immutable as the Laws of Cricket or the Landmarks of Freemasonry. There must be a kick-start. The wheels must be spoked, and (if you have pretensions to speed) they must also be alloy-rimmed. Twin-leading-shoe front brakes are superior to single-leading-shoe, both practically and aesthetically; though four-leading-shoe brakes are excessive, and you might as well use hydraulics. Needless to say, air scoops (with stone guards) are the acme of drum-brake design. The carburetter on a "soft" single may feed through an air-box, but on a proper parallel-twin or V-twin they should inhale through stubby ram stacks, again with a chrome-mesh stone-guard to keep out anything of pebble size or above. The silencers – or as Americans more accurately say, the *mufflers* – should have a certain note; neither too subdued nor (except in the case of a Goldie) too loud. The engine should not buzz or whine; each firing stroke should be heard, until the speed of the machine is such that the only sound is rolling thunder.

There is no need for such fripperies as electric turn signals, because the skilled traditionalist always gives hand signals (which are more often noticed, too), but the twist-grip must have an adjustable drag screw so that the throttle does not snap shut when you take your hand off the bars to signal or to wave to another rider. Mirrors are unnecessary; the rider glances behind him. The gear-lever, needless to say, is normally on the right.

The cylinders must be finned, the exhaust-pipe gleaming chrome, and the frame must be black. The paint must gleam; there must be chrome and polished light alloy. The wheels must be a respectable size, and the tyres must be in proportion – not huge hoops the size of an earth-mover's rubber, not as broad and slick as the tyres on last year's Formula One cars. The petrol tank must have petcocks, with a reserve position: no true motorcyclist trusts to fuel gauges. The only essential instrument is the legally-required speedometer: engine speed is gauged by ear, though a rev. counter is acceptable on *seriously* fast machinery, and an ammeter is not a bad idea if the electrics are Lucas or Miller. At least it gives you some warning of some kinds of electrical failure, and it helps you to position the piston(s) correctly for a kick-start.

With this quintessential motorcycle, the rider can diagnose his own problems, carry out his own maintenance. In a few minutes he can have the tank off, check the LT and HT connections, be sure there is fuel reaching the carburetters, see the spark. If there is fuel and a spark, the bike *has* to run: there's just no choice. The most modest tools are sufficient: half a dozen spanners, a plug wrench, a screwdriver and a pair of pliers. With tyre-irons, a patching kit and a pump clipped under the saddle, the rider need not even fear punctures.

Nor are these the only reasons for nostalgia. A classic motorcycle bespeaks a nobler age, when the sun never set on the British Empire and when Joe Lucas, the Prince of Darkness, was known and feared throughout the motorcycling world. An age when Americans with a hankering for a home-grown motorcycle were not restricted to a single antique design, which now sells as much on looks and sound as on function; and which most certainly does not sell at all on performance or handling. Or when, a little more recently, Harley-Davidson made a genuinely sporting motorcycle, the XLCR – which was roundly rejected by the American public, a generation of swine before whom such a pearl was cast. An age

BELOW: *BMW made their first shaft-drive, transverse, air-cooled flat twin in 1923 – the year this motorcycle was made – and they have stayed with the same layout ever since, despite their attempts* to shift the emphasis to their water-cooled triples and fours. BMW aficionados are more fiercely loyal to the brand than riders of almost any other make.

LEFT: *The 1926 Brough Superior SS100 was not quite the fastest machine of its day, but it came close. It was almost certainly the best-finished, though. The proprietary J.A.P. engine was specially made for the SS100; the cast fins on the exhaust pipes helped to dissipate what was at the time a tremendous amount of heat from an engine with a very high volumetric efficiency; and the wide, nickel-plated saddle tank set the fashion for decades to come. Both front and rear stands were provided, making it very easy to work on the motorcycle or to change a tyre. The SS100 was guaranteed to have been tested at more than 100 mph, in the days when most cars were hard put to exceed 60 mph.*

RIGHT: *The 1934 AJS R10 was a classic racer from the old-established firm of A.J. Stevens. All through the 1930s, and indeed well into the 1950s, British motorcycle manufacturers continued to refine the simple, elegant, lightweight 500cc single, persuading it to disburse more and more power while remaining wonderfully agile. Although power may be low by modern standards, so is weight; and riding an old 500cc single is a revelation to anyone used to overweight and over-complicated modern motorcycles.*

ABOVE: *The 1934 AJS at the top of the page might have found itself competing against the 1934 Norton Inter, above, which rapidly became the standard against which other singles were judged: for better than two decades, the "cammy" Norton was the ultimate single, challenged only by the DBD34 Goldie after World War Two. The "Brooklands can" silencer is typical of pre-war racers.*

of great V-twins from France and Switzerland and Czechoslovakia and Sweden; an age of Danish in-line fours and Italian singles where the cylinder was parallel with the ground and British flat fours and square fours and in-line fours. An age of magnetos and hand-controlled advance-retard levers and decompressors for starting big singles; an age of soaking chains in kerosene to clean them, then coiling them in the big, flat tins of grease that were designed to be heated on the stove for that very purpose.

For the *aficionado* with enough money, even the performance of those antique motorcycles can be impressive. The brake-horsepower figures may look low by modern standards, but they made up for it with immense torque, light weight, and a tiny frontal area. As early as the mid-to-late 1920s, there were a number of motorcycles that would exceed 100 mph (160 kph). The Brough SS100 was designed in 1923-1924, and was first offered for sale in the 1925 season; that is, late in 1924. It took its name from the fact that it was guaranteed, in writing, to be capable of exceeding 100 mph. Each motorcycle came with a test certificate, signed by the Brooklands track authorities, certifying that the fully-equipped machine (with tools, mudguards, etc.) had exceeded 100 mph for one kilometre.

And the SS100 was not even the fastest machine of the 1920s. The proprietary firm of Anzani (who supplied some engines for Broughs, though JAP motors were more usual) made road-going, 8-valve V-twins which were fitted both to the British McEvoy and the Austrian Krammer. In a day when side-valves were the norm, four-valve heads were extraordinary; but neither the McEvoy-Anzani nor the Krammer-Anzani lasted much more than half a decade. In any case, they were eclipsed first by the Brough Pendine, with its triple valve springs and 110 mph test certificate – that was in 1926 – and then by the 1934 New SS100. This was virtually a racing motorcycle in road trim, with twin carbs, twin magnetos, and an 8:1 compression ratio. From its 996 cc JAP engine, it was reputed to deliver 74 bhp, which is 4 bhp more than the most powerful production BMW litre-class Boxers of almost half a century later.

Then there was the Vincent, originally the HRD. From the reasonably quick 500cc single was developed the 1000cc Rapide V-twin. The original, pre-War Series A "Plumber's Nightmare" (so called from the plethora of external oil-lines) offered only 45 bhp, but in a motorcycle that weighed about 430 lb. (under 200 Kg) it was enough to propel the pilot to more than 110 mph/180 kph in top (fourth) gear, with almost 100 mph/160 kph available in third and about 80 mph/125 kph in second. There were no speed limits on the open road in those days ….

After World War Two, the Series B Rapide formed the basis of the legendary Black Shadow, a super-sports derivative with Comet cams, blueprinted and polished internals, 7.3:1 compression ratio instead of 6.6:1 (this was the era of rotten "pool" petrol), and the massive crank-cases enamelled a gleaming black. The 3-inch, 120-mph speedometer of the Rapide was replaced with an enormous 5-inch, 150-mph unit, though there was still no rev. counter: anyone who bought a Vincent was presumed capable of judging engine speed by ear. A freshly-fettled Shadow could hit 125 mph, just over the magic 200 kph; and this was in the late 1940s. For the ultimate Vincent, the engine could be taken to Black Lightning specification: 140 mph in normal use, though Rollie Free topped 150 mph in the course of a speed record attempt, lying full-length on the saddle and clad only in swimming trunks and running shoes … and this was all before 1950!

After the demise of the Vincent in 1955, British parallel twins ruled the roost; but then the Italians (who had always been interested in high-output, multiple-cylinder engines for racing) finally came out with the MV Agusta transverse four in road-going trim, well before the Honda 750 Four, and the writing was on the

wall for the V-twin. Then Benelli upped the ante with the *Sei*, a transverse six, and the world started to go to hell in a handbasket.

Few of us, though, can afford these machines today. Indeed, few have ever been able to afford them: they were always rare and expensive, though surprisingly untemperamental. So what are the attractions of more modest machinery?

Well, apart from all the "real motorcycle" attributes listed above, a major part of their charm is how very easy they can be to ride. Certainly, there were some machines which were downright rotten no matter how you rode them, and there were others which were only at home with a huge sidecar tacked on the side; a Watsonian Double Adult, the size of a beach hut and about as aerodynamic. The bike to tow one of these was a P&M Panther, the proverbial "big pussy" singles with an enormously long stroke and an engine which fired on passing every other lamp-post.

But a "cooking" single, such as an Enfield Clipper or even for that matter an Enfield Bullet, was a universal motorcycle such as we can hardly imagine today. The power output might be laughably low by modern standards, 25 bhp or less from a 500cc single; but it would pull you along at 80 to 85 mph (130-140 kph), and it would sip petrol at a miserly 60-70 mpg or even better (less than 4.5 litres/100 km). It would chug along at what would now be unbelievably low engine speeds, the big flywheel carrying you between the distinct, clearly-separated firing pulses, and you could ride it over almost anything: a standard, out-of-the-box

BELOW: *The Red Hunter – this one dates from 1938 – was one of the best-known motorcycles ever to be made* *by the old-established firm of Ariel, whose logo was a stylized (iron?) horse.*

LEFT AND BELOW: *Many devotees of American V-twins reckon that the Indian was always a better motorcycle than the Harley-Davidson, and that the wrong marque survived. That may be a bit harsh, but this 45-cubic-inch (740cc) Pony Scout from 1939 is a very fine motorcycle in its livery of traditional Indian red. It was, however, very old-fashioned even for 1939, with its foot clutch and hand gear-change, and cooling problems would soon result in narrow-angle air-cooled V-twins being abandoned for motorcycles with any pretensions to performance. Another Indian peculiarity was "wrong" (left-hand) throttle operation on some machines, allegedly to allow police riders to use their right hands for shooting while riding! One wonders if anyone ever actually tried this: it sounds excessively difficult.*

Bullet can take dried-up rice-paddies in its stride at 5 mph (10 kph), and will not twitch when you hit a pot-hole at ten times that speed. The "handling envelope" is so forgiving that you would have great difficulty in going too fast for the frame; the engine is just not powerful enough to get you into trouble. The Enfield was but one of many singles, such as the Matchless G80, the Norton ES2, or the BSA B-series.

Or again, the old, weird-looking Velocette LE-series "Noddy Bike" will carry you along in great comfort and enormous economy (albeit very slowly indeed) forever. The "LE" stands for "little engine," a tiny, water-cooled side-valve flat twin that started as a 150cc, grew to 175cc, and then hit 200cc in its final incarnation – in which form it was still hard-pressed to exceed 45 mph (say 75 kph). It is not a bike that many people would choose as a long-distance tourer, but it is still the ultimate commuter bike or runabout.

If you want something a bit more mainstream, there are endless derivatives of the original Speed Twin: not just the Bonnie, but the various BSA models (including the A-series), the Nortons (including the Atlas and the Commando), the Enfields (Meteor/Super Meteor, Constellation), Ariel, A.J.S., Matchless …. Believe it or not, these twins originally gained much of their popularity because they vibrated so much less than the big singles that they replaced, while delivering even more power. Power outputs were still very much lower than modern machines, at 30 to 35 bhp for all but the most powerful models, but at last the "ton" (100 mph/160 kph) was in sight for the ordinary motorcyclist. In the days when they were current, Triumphs were regarded as fastest, but with suspect handling, and Nortons were slower, but cornered like a ball-bearing in a groove; so the Triton, the Triumph engine in a Norton frame, provided the best of both worlds.

If you were a real purist, though, you might prefer to get your high-speed thrills from a really powerful single such as the immortal Goldie: 38 bhp, and an engine which flooded and died below 2000 rpm unless you blipped the throttle every few seconds, causing infants to whimper and windows to rattle.

Then, switching back to the unusual, you had another class of motorcycle which hardly exists today: the "gentleman's motorcycle," which was designed above all to be smooth but which would, if pushed, go surprisingly quickly. The Sunbeam S7 and S8, first introduced in the late 1940s, were equipped with parallel twins mounted longitudinally in the frame (not transversely!) and were one example; the "Squariel" or Ariel Square Four was another. The Square Four was essentially two parallel twins with their crankshafts geared together: smooth and powerful, but prone to overheating at the rear if pushed too hard for too long. This was also a besetting fault of the in-line

RIGHT: *The tank badges reveal that this is an original Royal Enfield – not a modern Indian-built Enfield, which is a current production bike that is almost identical to the British motorcycle, having continued in production long after the British parent company disappeared. It is an interesting question which is more desirable: the "real thing," like Bryan Amos's bike here, or the Indian copy which has had the benefit of four decades of additional development, albeit often at a somewhat leisurely pace. Both British and Indian Bullets are available in either 350cc or 500cc guise, and to the power-crazed modern rider, even the 500 will seem modest enough; but both motorcycles are incredibly strong, and have frames which can very easily handle all the modest power that is available. This means that you have to be very careless indeed to get yourself in trouble, which makes the Bullet a very safe motorcycle as well as a very reliable one.*

Sunbeams, and it was what killed the longitudinally-mounted in-line fours which had begun in the first decade of the century with the 363cc FN and which had persisted in such models as the (Indian) Ace, the Henderson Four, and the Nimbus. Modern gentlemen may still ride motorcycles, but they demand powerful machines where the power can really be used.

Or if character and originality above all were what you craved, you could have the two-stroke Scott – very quick when it ran, which was by no means all the time – or the Austin-engined, four-cylinder Brough Superior with the twin rear wheels (for sidecar use only!) or even the five-cylinder radial-engined Megola ….

Perhaps, though, your taste runs more to "instant nostalgia" and to bikes built the way that bikes were always built. Better metallurgy, maybe, and better breathing and more economical carburetters, and brakes that work (something which can by no means be taken for granted with older machines), but still looking like real motorcycles complete with daylight showing through the frame. Well, you have plenty of choice there, too.

The ultimate nostalgia bike, as already intimated above, is the Bullet from The Enfield India. This is essentially an early-to-mid-1950s motorcycle with some (but not all) of the bugs ironed out. It still vibrates like a good 'un, and even the 500cc model

ABOVE: *The Brough SS80 preceded the SS100, and was guaranteed in writing to have exceeded 80 mph. When it was introduced, Queen Victoria had been dead for only two decades. After the overhead-valve SS100 came out, the side-valve SS80 (with its "fir-cone" caps over the valves) remained in production for those who wanted a more tractable, traditional machine. Because it is so greatly overshadowed by the SS100, it remains (relatively) affordable; and apart from the rather puny brakes, it is still a great pleasure to ride.*

RIGHT: *The twin-rear-wheel Brough Superior is a rare sight at the best of times; shorn of its side-car, it is even rarer. It is presumably possible to ride the beast solo, though it is hard to imagine anyone being rash enough to attempt it.*

This Brough, powered by a four-cylinder engine borrowed from the Austin Seven, was only one of many special and show motorcycles built by George Brough, but unlike most of them it actually made it into a limited production run of a handful of motorcycles.

(reintroduced in 1990 after nearly four decades of 350s) is hardly a road-burner at 22 bhp. But it is oil-tight, and it sounds right, and it looks right, and it is even priced right; it is one of the most reasonably-priced motorcycles on the market. There is a factory prototype with an overhead cam, and the chief engineer does not rule out a four-valve head …. The days of the 100 mph classic single may yet return.

Half the world away, the Harley-Davidson is hardly any more advanced; instead of being a (marginally) updated 1950s motorcycle, it is a (marginally) updated 1930s motorcycle. It does not even have the offset cylinder design which has been *de rigeur* in fast V-twins at least since 1936: no, the cylinders are mounted in line, and the con-rods are of the "knife and fork" style of the earliest Harleys from the first decade of the twentieth century. The rear cylinder of the narrow-angle, air-cooled engine would probably cook if anyone rode these behemoths flat out, but that is not what owning a Harley is about. Like the Bullet, it is about sounding right, looking right, and being the kind of vintage technology that just about anyone can understand. The monster pistons mean that even the baby 900cc machines vibrate spectacularly, while the big "eighty inch" (1340cc) engines are like cement mixers. But if nostalgia is your bag ….

The third "instant nostalgia" bike is the BMW Boxer. This is actually an updated 1920s motorcycle, but it was a superior design to the Harley to start with and it has been able to withstand a great deal more updating. Having the cylinders sticking out into the air flow means that cooling is not a problem; vibration is very much less, because of the "boxer" movement of the pistons; and although the float-bowls of the carburetters get in the way of the rider's feet, they are nothing like as inconvenient as the Harley's inhalation arrangements. Every BMW lover has his or her own favourite BMW, but strong contenders are the old, low-saddle black models with the white pin-stripes; the R90S, the first BMW "Hyperbike"; and the early R100RS, with the most powerful production boxer motor ever built (70 bhp instead of the later models' 60 bhp) and the most beautiful fairing ever devised for a motorcycle.

And then, in very limited production at Easton Neston, there is the Hesketh V1000; a gentleman's superbike in the tradition of

ABOVE: *This 1949 Vincent Black Lightning is the actual machine on which Rollie Free took the world motorcycle speed record, lying full-length on the saddle. Note the extensive "added lightness" achieved by drilling holes wherever possible – and note how close this record-breaker is to a standard, road-going Vincent.*

BELOW: *The Mark II "Squariel," with its all-alloy engine, was designed for relaxed high-speed cruising with plenty of power in reserve for overtaking, but improved roads meant that too many people treated the overtaking speed as the cruising speed, usually "cooking" the rear cylinders in the process.*

the Brough SS100 and the Vincent Black Shadow, a mighty 1000cc V-twin finished to the very highest standards, but unfortunately carrying a price to match. Even at that, the price was only comparable with an immaculate Vincent .... The manufacturers once called it "The Last 1950s Motorcycle."

With almost a century of delectable machinery to choose from, what are the advantages and drawbacks of riding "real" motorcycles, and what should you look for?

The advantages of nostalgic motorcycles are simple to describe, and surprisingly numerous. There is the pleasure of owning a classic, of standing out from the crowd. For the most part, unless you buy the most rip-roaring motorcycles such as a Brough New SS100 or a Vincent with a Lightning-specification engine, they are surprisingly easy to ride and to keep in adjustment. Because of the lower power outputs, even large-capacity machines are often surprisingly light by modern standards: a 500cc motorcycle from the days of the Great War might weigh as little as 220 lb (100 Kg), while the mighty Vincent is well under 500 lb. This light weight and "soft" power delivery makes them very relaxing to ride.

They will go almost anywhere, because the roads of the past were often far worse than the roads of today. They are remarkably undemanding; many a classic motorcycle is perfectly practical everyday transport. And if you choose a classic from the 1950s or 1960s, you may well find that modern tyres give you handling such as many people can only dream of: a Norton Featherbed running on modern Avons is a joy forever.

The disadvantages are about equally numerous. The most significant, on the vast majority of older machines, is the abysmal quality of the brakes – and the older they are, the worse the brakes. Motorcycles capable of 100 mph (160 kph) or more were fitted with brakes which would now be regarded as insufficient for a commuter bike: on the less crowded roads of the past, people apparently did not worry about such things so much.

The other area in which serious shortcomings may be apparent is in the electrics. Six-volt systems, tiny batteries and feeble

ABOVE AND BELOW: *The R69S, in its sober pin-striped black livery and with the front end sprung on Earles forks, is now seen as a classic – but it was very nearly the death of BMW. In its time, the single-carb twin was seen as overweight, over-priced, underpowered and unexciting. The improbable "flying" seat, separate pillion, and idiosyncratic rear suspension only made it look more old-fashioned, which is part of its charm today.*

FACING PAGE: *"Mud plugging" on a classic trials bike like this old BSA can be just as much fun as it was when the bike was new; and some people prefer a "real" motorcycle to a modern off-road machine with its enormous seat height, long front forks, and buzz-saw engine note. It cannot compete with new bikes; so don't race it against new bikes! Also, skills learned on an old bike can be applied to newer machines; the reverse is not always true.*

headlamps were not much fun when the machines were new; with decades of corrosion and bodged wiring repairs, they can be a nightmare today. Many owners of really old motorcycles will ride only during the day.

Although classic motorcycles are mostly mechanically simple, parts may or may not be available. For a few selected makes, especially Vincents and Triumph twins, parts may actually be easier to find (and sometimes cheaper) than parts for new Japanese or Italian superbikes; but if your Levis needs a new piston, or your Victoria is missing its front mudguard, finding the part you want may be difficult or impossible, and you may have to resort to getting parts made. As with the wiring, you may find that previous owners have bodged repairs and, if they have, life can get very depressing indeed, with whole hubs being replaced because of stripped and cross-threaded bolts, or "standard" parts suddenly refusing to fit because the part that they bolt onto has been modified.

Unless you like working on motorcycles more than you like riding them, you would therefore do best to look for a machine which is in full running order *and* which offers ready availability of parts. The "instant nostalgia" bikes like the Indian Enfield, Harley-Davidson, BMW and Hesketh are ideal for this (though the price of parts varies widely!), but Nortons, Triumphs and BSAs are not far behind, and the more dedicated owners' clubs have parts manufactured in batches; the Vincent Owners' Club is particularly noted for this.

There are many mansions in the house of classic-bike fanciers, from the obsessive concours contestants to the vintage racers and those who like touring on classic motorcycles, which can handle low-octane petrol and low-tech maintenance in the still-backward countries of Eastern Europe or in the wilds of, say, Turkey. There are indeed many riders who only like to ride for short distances on a fine Sunday, reserving a more modern (and possibly more reliable) motorcycle for the majority of their riding. But the intriguing thing is that while many people may change their modern motorcycles as often as they can afford it or as often as they feel inclined, vintage machines and their riders tend to grow old together; and it is sadly true that often, it is only when an old man dies that another carefully-tended Brough Superior, or Vincent Rapide, or Sunbeam single comes on the market.

It is hard to believe that the "ugly duckling" Velocette LE 200 (inset right) came from the same nest as the clutch of swans below. On the other hand, much as variations on the theme of a light, slim, fast 500cc single may be what we associate with the last days of Velocette, the men from Hall Green were quite correct to realise that they needed to diversify if they were to survive. The LE 200 is arguably the finest commuter bike ever made: superbly stable, wonderfully reliable and economical to run, and even providing a radiator on which to warm your hands in cold weather. A beautifully made shaft-drive flat twin was, however, too expensive and too heavy to compete with the likes of the Honda 50 and Honda 90 and in the long run the 500cc singles were simply rendered obsolete by much more powerful parallel twins.

ABOVE: *The 1953 Ariel Mk. II Square Four was a solution in search of a problem. Inevitably heavy, complex and expensive to manufacture, it simply did not provide the kind of all-out performance that people expected from a machine of that capacity and in that price range. Even so, there are to this day people who maintain that the Squariel is one of the finest bikes ever built.*

RIGHT: *God may ride a Harley, but Jesus prefers Sunbeams. By 1953, when the S8 was produced, the proud name of Sunbeam was definitely in decline. Like the Squariel (and for much the same reasons) the Sunbeam longitudinal twins suffered from overheating rear cylinders, and people simply rode them harder than they could be ridden. Also, a fatally weak final drive meant that a sports 'Beam was not practical.*

ABOVE: In anyone's list of all-time classics, the Black Shadow must be at or very close to the top: other contenders include the Brough Superior and (arguably) the Hesketh, all massive V-twins, all staggeringly handsome, and all rather alarmingly expensive. Despite the increasing tendency to call all Vincents "Shadows," it is easy to tell a Shadow from a Rapide. The Shadow has black enamelled crank cases, while the Rapide's are bright alloy.

BELOW: It is simply untrue that all British manufacturers were reactionary and determined to cling to obsolete designs, as this 1954 "triple knocker" AJS from Team Obsolete shows. What happened was that throughout the 1940s and 1950s, accountants increasingly took over from enthusiasts, and "state of the art" designs were vetoed by bean counters who understood nothing about motorcycles and the people who rode them.

FACING PAGE AND RIGHT: *Most people remember Matchless as a purveyor of somewhat stolid singles; but they also had their moments of glory. The extremely purposeful G50 racer on the left, with its twin-leading-shoe brakes and open primary drive, dates from 1955 and is one example. And it would be interesting to know if someone from Plumstead Road devised the wonderful 1952 "Valentine" advertisement, or whether they employed an advertising agency. One rather expects it was an "in-house" idea: it is a lovely mixture of naivety, enthusiasm, and tongue-in-cheek humour, even if the motorcycle in question is one of the "stolid singles" mentioned above. Strangely enough, the Matchless name was one of the few to be rescued from the AMC empire: you can still find modern Matchless G80 singles, with proprietary engines, today.*

14th February 1952
Oh would that I could make you mine My longed-for Matchless Valentine

MATCHLESS MOTOR CYCLES · PLUMSTEAD ROAD · LONDON, S.E.18 · ENGLAND

LEFT: *It may seem strange that the G50 was a single while the G45 was a twin, but that is the way it was. This 1955 G45 racer has the characteristic open primary drive, in the interests of cooling, accessibility and weight saving: note also the cooling holes drilled at the front of the somewhat rudimentary guard for the primary chain.*

While there is no doubt that this motorcycle would be hopelessly outclassed by a modern machine of similar displacement, it is equally undeniable that the simple, classic lines of the Matchless have an aesthetic purity which is conspicuously absent from a modern fully-faired, graphics-strewn "Ricky Racer" equivalent. This is a motorcycle that looks like a motorcycle – and a very handsome motorcycle at that.

ABOVE: *This 1955 Black Prince, Vincent's swan-song, is said by some to have been a money-saving exercise: it was allegedly cheaper to* swathe the motorcycle in fibreglass than to finish the individual parts to the kind of standard Vincent deemed necessary. On the other hand, it looks handsome, and it does indeed bring to mind a medieval knight's charger caparisoned for war. This example would look better if the stripe were the original gold leaf, rather than yellow paint.

RIGHT: *the DBD34 "Goldie" – BSA's Gold Star – was an awful motorcycle to ride in town. The noise was shattering, the throttle had to be blipped constantly to keep the engine alight, and reliability was dubious in the extreme. But on the open road...Ahhhh...*

BELOW: *the AJS 7R "Boy's Racer" was a racer which could be made street-legal. It was called the "boy's" racer because it was a 350 – a "boy's" bike rather than a "man's" 500 – but its light weight and precise handling remain legendary even today. Looking at it closely, you realise how extraordinarily light and slim it is.*

LEFT AND FACING PAGE TOP: *Norton's ES2 (left) was a prime example of the "cooking" or "ride-to-work" pushrod singles which provided the company's bread and butter throughout the 1950s; this one dates from about 1956. But the fame of Norton singles did not rest on pushrod engines: rather, it was the "cammy" or "double-knocker" machines like the Inter (right). With the light, powerful 500cc single mounted in the double-loop "featherbed" frame and (of course) twin-leading-shoe brakes and alloy rims, the Inter was a prime example of the ultimate development of the 500cc single, before big singles were toppled from their long-held position of racing supremacy and everyday convenience, yielding first to twins and then to fours. Even today, though, big singles still have their devotees*

LEFT AND RIGHT: *Norton's 750cc Atlas – this one dates from 1964 – was very much more powerful than the old singles: with twice as many cylinders, and fifty per cent more swept volume, it could hardly be otherwise. With Norton's double-loop frame and Roadholder forks, it also handled in an exemplary fashion. On the debit side, it had a ferocious tendency to vibration, shaking the fillings loose from its riders' teeth. In the early 1970s, before the Atlas achieved classic status, it was not a very popular second-hand machine. In truth, 750cc is too big for a highly-stressed parallel twin: a 650cc twin is much smoother, and a 500cc twin is a delight. But motorcyclists keep demanding more and more power, and a bigger and bigger engine is the easiest (if not the best) way to give it to them.*

ABOVE: *the heart of the matter, the engine of a DBD34 "Goldie," with its open ram-stack carburettor which was little more than an open tube pouring neat fuel into the inlet tract. Below 2000 rpm, even the roadgoing Gold Star was inclined to baulk; and in Clubman's trim, with the racing carb, low-speed tractability was non-existent. This one dates from 1960, a very late example.*

RIGHT: *Velocette must have made the loveliest-looking 350cc and 500cc singles of all time – even if the clutches were not easy to adjust. As the men at Hall Green extracted more and more power from the elderly single, it acquired more and more names: this is a Thruxton (named after the race-track) Venom, and dates from 1966, just before Velocettes finally disappeared.*

FACING PAGE TOP RIGHT: *BSA's A65 Spitfire – this one is to UK specification and dates from the 1960s – is a fine old machine, but illustrates very well why the Japanese took over the motorcycle business. By the 1960s, true innovation had been almost entirely crushed by the dead hand of accountants, and while an evolutionary process of design ensured that British motorcycles got better and better, they were evolving in a dead-end: lighter, faster motorcycles with higher-revving, higher-tech overhead cam engines were the wave of the future.*

It is also important to remember that the British were only one casualty of the motorcycle wars: the French, the Swiss, the Germans (with the exception of BMW) had all succumbed earlier, and all had had flourishing motorcycle industries at one time.

BELOW AND LEFT: *The 600cc Phelon and Moore Panther 100 – the "Big Pussy" – was the last of the big, soft, sidecar-pulling singles. By 1960, when this one was made, it was an anachronism, with a tiny market niche. The aim of the manufacturers, maximum torque rather than maximum power, is clear from the relatively tiny carburettor on the enormously long-stroke cylinder, which also serves as the front down-tube on the frame. The sound of a Panther thumping through the early evening, each firing stroke clearly distinguishable from the next, is a sound which motorcyclists of a certain age will always remember. Often, the Panther was used to pull "commercial" side-cars; it was much favoured by window-cleaners and chimney-sweeps.*

LEFT: *The Hesketh V1000 is a modern, 90-degree V-twin built to the highest possible standards: not just an immaculate finish, but also designed for longevity. Some parts are so massive and understressed that they will not wear significantly across the entire life of the motorcycle: others, which necessarily must wear, are designed to be replaced when at last it becomes imperative. There is room in the cylinder walls for ten overbores, for example. The only disadvantage of the Hesketh, as with the Vincent before it and the Brough Superior before that, is that it is a very expensive motor-cycle. Arguably, even more than Brough, it deserves the title "The Rolls-Royce of Motorcycles" – and the price per kilogram (a surprisingly accurate guide to mechanical quality) is roughly the same as for a Rolls – Royce.*

ABOVE AND FACING PAGE BOTTOM: At a gathering of the Norton Owners' Club (above), a concours d'elegance of Commandos displays considerable variation in detail and personal taste. The Commando, last of Norton's big twins, enjoys a mixed reputation. A poorly maintained example is without doubt unreliable and unpleasant to ride, but if you look after a Commando it will reward you with superb handling, excellent reliability, and a turn of speed which is very respectable even today. The machine on the left is Paul Thomas's 1975 M3, which had 100,000 miles (160,000 kilometres) under its wheels when it was photographed here as "Best Overall" at the show. The actual swept volume is 828cc, and the "Electric Start" is best regarded as power assistance for the kick-start.

LEFT AND ABOVE: *MV Agusta is known for helicopters and motorcycles, an unusual combination, but the rare, expensive MV reflects its aerospace heritage in its excellent materials, build quality and quality control. An early devotee of the transverse-four layout, the Agusta provides extraordinary handling and (for its time) very considerable power – these motorcycles are the Ferraris of the two-wheel world. This is a 1977 America 750cc – a very lean, spare machine despite its apparently all-enveloping bodywork, which in truth is a remarkably thin shell. Closer contemplation of the Agusta reveals why the Japanese conquered the four-cylinder market, too. The Italian bike embodies few compromises: it is a determinedly lightweight semi-racer, effectively built in a racing shop, so the price was very high indeed. The four-cylinder "UJM" (Universal Japanese Motorcycle), on the other hand, correctly gauged that as a selling point power is more important than handling or weight; and power at a low price will always sell, regardless of any other deficiencies that the machine may have.*

RIGHT: *Those who do not ride Harley-Davidsons always have mixed feelings about them. On the one hand, there is no doubt that they look and sound wonderful. The whole machine is readily comprehensible, and is made up of sensible pieces: this bolts to that, which screws to this, which bolts to that. The ragged, deep-chested beat of the 45-degree V-twin, a result of a wildly uneven firing interval, is unmistakable. On the other hand, very few Harleys can be ridden fast: this 1979 Super Glide is better than some, because it has foot pegs rather than foot boards, which ground under all but the gentlest cornering, but the huge, heavy engine in a huge, heavy frame does not make for a nimble motorcycle. Also, the tiny size of most Harley-Davidson petrol tanks (the smallest are only about four litres) argues strongly that many Harley-Davidson riders are more interested in posing than in riding any distance. Then again, the vibration from a Harley engine, especially the big 80-inch models, makes riding at 60-70 mph a penance: even with the Evo engine, the vibration can shake your eyeballs in their sockets so badly that you cannot read road signs.*

RIGHT: *The Benelli 750 Sei (right) was the world's first production six-cylinder roadster; but it was never particularly successful, commercially or otherwise. Italian electrics and Italian paint were a part of the problem, and the engine never delivered as much power as everyone thought it should.*

BELOW: *The R90S (the 1976 model below is in "Daytona Orange") was BMW's first "superbike," with a top speed, if you were lucky, of 200 kph (124 mph). Purists moaned and said that 900cc was too big for the old Boxer, but everyone agreed that the airbrushed paint job was stunning, and the "bikini" fairing started a fashion.*

LEFT: *Harley-Davidsons always lend themselves to "dressing up" with lots of chrome and accessories, and this 1976 Electra Glide FLH is no exception. It is, however, an almost unbelievably old-fashioned motorcycle, right down to the huge single seat, the all-chrome tank, and the positioning of the instruments. On any modern motorcycle the instruments are situated where the rider can see them without having to take his eyes off the road: a tank-mounted speedo, on the other hand, is down-right dangerous. The "fat bob" tank is effectively two pannier tanks instead of one saddle tank, which is also fairly eccentric, but at least it holds a reasonable amount of fuel – about as much as the smallest BMW tank.*

FACING PAGE BOTTOM: *Compare the Hesketh with the Harley-Davidson above it. Both are massive V-twins, but they are decades apart in design philosophy. The admittedly heavy Hesketh is lighter,* *more powerful, faster, better-braked, better cooled, and somehow more elegant than the Harley; the contrast is akin to that between a Rolls Royce and a Mack truck.*

ABOVE: *Now compare the Honda XBR500 with both the Harley and the Hesketh opposite. It is undoubtedly superb value for money, and the rather hunch-backed tank has a certain functional* *charm; if it were not for the extraordinarily hideous wheels, this might be the modern lightweight sports classic that Honda presumably intended.*

The Harley engine on the left dates from 1992; the bike facing page below, from 1982; and the one facing page above is an elderly flat-head (side-valve) of uncertain vintage spotted at Daytona in 1984. The family resemblance between all three is unmistakable, and Harley-Davidson has done its best to blur the line between past and present with its Softail, which looks like a rigid frame but actually incorporates rear suspension.

While no-one would begrudge Harley-Davidson their hard-earned success, it is difficult not to fantasize about what other makes would have been like if they had survived, and to wonder, for that matter, whether they might not have been better motorcycles than Harley-Davidson. What might the Swiss Condor have been like? Or the British Vincent? Or the American Indian, for that matter?

What is the correct blend of tradition and innovation? Is the narrow-angle V-twin, with its inherent cooling problems and its antiquated knife-and-fork connecting rods, totally obsolete and fit only for the scrap heap? Or is it what it has always been, a big, solid, torquey engine whose sporting pretensions ceased decades ago?

Then again, perhaps even those speculations are too negative. Perhaps those of us who love proper, traditional motorcycles should just be grateful that we still have Harley-Davidsons, and Indian Enfields, and BMW Boxers and Heskeths and Matchless G80s, and even Norton rotaries; for even they, in their way, are that precious blend of old and new that makes a classic

2 DIRT

Nobody in their right mind would imagine you could *walk* through the course. Short but steep, muddy hills would have you on your hands and knees in no time. A stream-bed, strewn with everything from pebbles to boulders, looks ready to break your ankle if you try to cross it on foot – if the icy water doesn't sweep away your footing first. The few stretches of what might optimistically be called roadway (or at least pathway) are so rutted that you realize the Army knew what it was doing when it issued you with those huge, horrible boots. A tree the size of Yggdrasil has fallen across one of them; with mountain-climbers' crampons you might just about be able to scramble across its mossy, slimy trunk.

Then you hear a sound like a slightly asthmatic buzz-saw, and a tall, skinny-tyred motorcycle comes into view. It is moving surprisingly slowly. The rider, a look of fierce concentration on his face and a somewhat abbreviated helmet on his head, is standing on the footrests. Like a chess-player in a time-lapse movie, he picks his course through the stream; avoiding some rocks, climbing over others, shifting his body weight to keep the centre of gravity just so. Before you realize it, he is across: or rather, he has ridden into the stream, up it for a few metres, then out on the other size. He seems hardly to have rippled the water. You think of the master butcher of Chinese legend, whose knives never needed sharpening because he always cut in precisely the right place.

The engine screams briefly as the rider rears the bike up on its back wheel; surely he is going to be left astride that tree-trunk with both wheels in the air. But no, the enormously long suspension comes into play, and he scrabbles and is over, heading for the hill. Now the engine note rises as he charges the muddy bank. Almost at the top, his rear wheel begins to go sideways, but by a combination of throttle control and countersteering he makes it. He is lost from view, but another engine-note is already growling on the far side of the creek.

LEFT: *Arthur Stubbs on a 1964 DOT 250 leads Pete Alleborne on an old 250 Cotton – a useful reminder that it is not just modern bikes that can be persuaded to cross difficult terrain.*
ABOVE: *flat-track racing gives quite another meaning to riding on dirt.*

LEFT: *Off-road bikes used to be nothing more than lightly-modified road bikes: knobbly tyres, a little more clearance on the front mudguard, but few other changes. This 1948 Triumph Trophy even has rubber foot-rests and a luggage rack on the tank – and a rigid rear end, which would give pause to anyone brought up with modern trial bikes!*

FACING PAGE: *"Green-laning" – riding non-competitively on dirt roads and trails – is much less stressful on both bike and rider than "full chat" racing on modern dirt bikes. A "soft" old four-stroke allows you time to listen to birdsong, and breathe the sweet air, without really disrupting the peace of the countryside.*

Most of the world calls it "Moto-Cross," but the old English name is more descriptive; until the sixties, and even the seventies, it was called "Scrambles" or "Scrambling." There is something about the world "scramble" that is almost onomatopoeic, a desperate struggle for footing on a slippery surface, a clawing for grip. That's what moto-cross is about.

The rules are simple. Get from A to B without putting a foot down ("dabbing"), or worse still falling off. The person who does it fastest – or in some cases the person who does it at all – is the winner.

The motorcycles are simple, too, though increasingly specialized. For a traditional scramble you don't need a lot of power, but you do need a lot of torque. In particular, you need torque low down in the rev. range, for clambering across terrain where any normal motorcycle would stall. For most purposes a single-cylinder machine is plenty, though some singles are big: 600cc, or even bigger. A big flywheel helps to smooth out the torque, but it mustn't be too big or the throttle response would be too slow.

Exhaust pipes are carried high; this not only stops them being blocked by mud, but it also stops them filling up with water as you cross streams. To save you from burning yourself, they are often protected with heat-shields. There is no rubber on the footrests; that would be too slippery. Instead, there are metal teeth that look like something off a bear trap.

The wheels are traditional, wire-laced spoked wheels: heavier than cast alloy, but more flexible and less likely to be damaged by rocks and spills. If they are damaged, they can be repaired; a one-piece cast wheel cannot. They are shod with "knobblies" – blocky-tread tyres which would weave and squirm at any speed on the highway, but which do not fill up with mud and become useless, slippery discs when you leave the road. Brakes are rudimentary: tiny drums which look like something from a past era. Disc brakes may dry out faster if you get them wet, and they can certainly provide more stopping power; but drum brakes can stand a lot more mud and dirt. The suspension is very long and

very soft; useless for high-speed "flicking" on twisty backroads, but optimized for off-road use. Ground clearance is enormous, and seats are very high: short riders will be quite unable to touch the ground with both feet.

Wide bars provide both delicate control and massive leverage, as well as damping potential wobbles. Stone-guards protect the headlamp; some riders have stone-shields over the handlebar grips, too. On some motorcycles the chain is protected by plastic tubing, but on others it is left out in the open to take its chances with the mud and gravel and dust and water; chain life on dirt bikes is short. A very few off-road bikes have shaft drive; an advantage of chains is that you can change the rear sprocket, and hence the final drive ratio, quickly and easily.

Believe it or not, there are even people who tackle this sort of terrain – especially the muddy bits – with sidecars attached. The sidecars are even more basic than the motorcycles: tubular-metal frames with the merest minimum of sheet-alloy to protect the passenger from the mud and from flung-up stones. The sidecar passenger needs nerves of steel, and preferably a body of much the same material, because it is his job to throw himself around like a monkey on a stick in an attempt to keep all three wheels on the ground and the whole outfit from tipping over, but such men exist ….

There are two, or possibly three, styles of riding in the dirt. One, the oldest, is the sort already described: slow and considered, but traversing terrain which most people would regard as impossible. This is very much the British and European tradition. The second consists of riding across much easier terrain, but correspondingly faster: the course is "off-road," but the obstacles are fewer, further between, and usually less demanding. The second kind is very much more dangerous than the first, because even a rider of limited skill can bowl along at a fine speed until the unexpected happens, at which point he (or more rarely she) falls off and hits the ground very hard indeed. Skilled riders may make fewer mistakes, but they run the risk of hitting the ground just as hard. This is the American tradition. It is this second, or

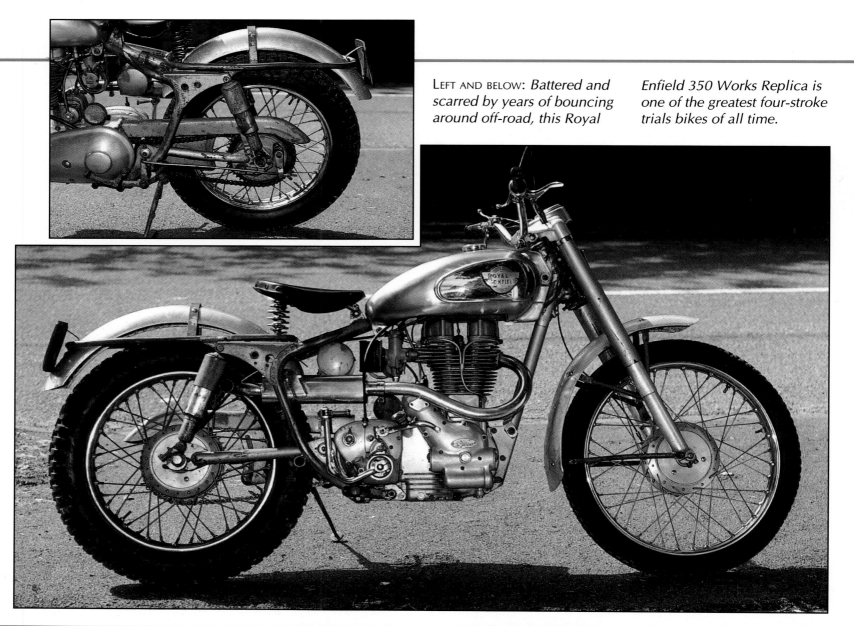

LEFT AND BELOW: *Battered and scarred by years of bouncing around off-road, this Royal Enfield 350 Works Replica is one of the greatest four-stroke trials bikes of all time.*

RIGHT: *In the 1950s and 1960s, when the motorcycles on the right were built, both Matchless and AJS were a part of AMC. Although suspension travel is negligible by modern standards, these machines could still traverse the most remarkable terrain – and of course parts are more readily available today for these decades-old machines than they are for some very much more modern motorcycles. On most week-ends, rain or shine, bikes like this will still be competing in scrambles all over Britain, and a few survive in use in the United States as well.*

FACING PAGE BOTTOM: *To the modern eye, one of the strange things about some old off-road bikes is how dapper they look: the elegantly black-enamelled tank of this 1961 AJS, with its gold-leaf lettering and pin-striping, would be more at home in a* concours d'elegance *than thrashing through the mud. Also, the modest clearance between the front wheel and its mudguard make you wonder how much of the gap that you find on modern bikes is strictly necessary, and how much is pure fashion.*

American, style of riding which spawned the body-armour business, with Kevlar-reinforced fabric and armoured plastic inserts at the elbows, knees and hips; with the old moto-cross style of riding, you seldom fell off at a high enough speed to make such things necessary.

Paradoxically, the greatest American-style race is held in Africa and is usually won by European riders. It is the Paris-Dakar, an alarmingly expensive and very dangerous race which is now the Paris-Capetown, about 7700 miles (almost 12,500 km). The European leg is nothing too remarkable, but the leg on the Dark Continent is fast, furious, and commonly fatal for at least one rider. Paris-Dakar motorcycles are like ordinary dirt bikes, only

more: the BMW R80G/S and R100G/S are big Boxers that have been modified to run very quickly off the road as well as on it, and other manufacturers have offered big V-twins, monster singles, and the occasional parallel twin. Gigantic fuel tanks, holding eight gallons or more, take care of the shortage of friendly neighbourhood gasoline stations in much of Africa.

For a certain type of rider, the Paris-Dakar Replica is the ultimate urban motorcycle. In Paris in particular, you see these massive and brightly-painted machines parked on the Champs-Elysees. It is clear that they have never been into the dirt; indeed, many of them have probably never been into *les banlieus*, the suburbs which a true Parisian regards as only slightly less exotic, risky and barbaric than the wilder parts of *l'Afrique*. In many ways, the riders of these apparently over-specialized machines have the right idea, though. After all, urban speeds are generally low – it is hard to do much more than sixty miles an hour (100 kph) down the Champs Elysees – and the low-speed "flickability" that the wide bars confer is exactly what you need for weaving through dense traffic. Add to this the potholes that plague even the finest cities, and the fact that a Paris-Dakar Replica is built to take knocks that would require expensive cosmetic surgery on any other high-profile machine, and maybe they have the right idea after all.

But these Parisian daredevils (or poseurs) are not exponents of the possible third style of off-road riding mentioned above. No; by that I meant a style which combines both the European and the American traditions, but applies it quite differently. For want of a better term, you might call it "exploratory touring."

If you were brave enough, you could probably do it with a luxo-tourer – a Venture or a Honda Goldwing. What you really need, though, is a bike that's light enough to pick up when it falls over, and where a "dab" (putting your foot down to steady yourself) won't break your ankle or your leg. You need enough power for the roadgoing parts, however, or you will get bored as you trundle down the highway being overtaken by milk floats, elderly ladies in Cadillacs, and Wartburgs. A 350 is the minimum you can conveniently get by with; a big "dual-sport" BMW R100G/S or R80G/S is probably the maximum.

Ideally, the scenario goes like this. First, you pick a country where even the paved roads are not necessarily going to be all that good: Portugal, Greece, Eastern Europe, India. The soft suspension of your "dual-sport" bike will be essential to soak up the potholes. Then, as the fancy takes you, you start to explore the side-roads. You will encounter alarming cambers, evil gravel surfaces, animals asleep in the road, children playing; but you will start to see the country as few tourists see it.

Inevitably, sooner or later, some of these side-roads turn into back roads; and the back roads turn into tracks; and the tracks turn into paths; and you may even run out of road entirely.

The point at which you turn back is up to you, but it is worth pointing out that almost any motorcycle can handle far worse conditions than might be thought possible. A fully-laden touring motorcycle, two-up, can handle tracks and paths that would defy or bog almost any four-wheeled vehicle; but it is worth reiterating that sooner or later there comes a point where a given combination of machine and terrain will be physically too much to handle. If you have the body of a giant, and the physique of a weight-lifter, you may regard a Harley-Davidson as a perfectly suitable motorcycle for off-road exploration, but if not there are going to be limits to the size of the motorcycle that you can manhandle.

Maybe there are four styles of off-road riding, at that; the three already mentioned, and a fourth – principally American – where you take your bike to where the road ends, either on a trailer or in the back of a van or pick-up truck, then strike off into the boonies.

RIGHT: *It is interesting that the Americans, whose normal preference for enormously heavy motorcycles is so well known, are so addicted to lightweight off-road bikes such as this Suzuki 125X, while the Europeans buy the big Paris-Dakar replicas. Perhaps it is because the price of these machines is relatively low in the United States, and they can easily be loaded into the back of a pick-up truck and carried to where they are to be ridden. Bigger bikes, even 350cc machines, typically need specialized bike trailers, or even have to be ridden from A to B under their own power.*

LEFT: *It is hard to believe that the spindly, almost toy-like Montesa Cota 310 (this is a 1990 model) is a serious off-road machine; but it is, and a very competitive one at that. On a purpose-built off-road machine, small fuel tanks are the norm, as this means less fuel to be spilled in the event of a fall. Note the breather on top of the tank.*

ABOVE: *There are distinct differences of style between European off-road machines such as this 1987 Beta TR34 from Italy and Japanese bikes. Paradoxically, it is the Japanese machines which tend to look old-fashioned, while low seat heights make the European bikes easier to ride.*

RIGHT: *Today, "high-tech" makes its appearance even in off-road bikes, like this 1990 Beta with its aluminium-girder frame and liquid-cooled engine. To a traditionalist, liquid-cooling a trials bike is almost inconceivable, but it certainly works, as more and more liquid-cooled engines testify.*

ABOVE: *In the specialized world of competitive enduro and moto-cross riding, all kinds of makers can challenge the giant Japanese manufacturers. This 1991 KTM 600 sports a liquid-cooled motor, an ultra-high-level exhaust and enormous suspension travel, and a sticker on the swinging arm proudly proclaims KTM's competition record: "2X ENDURO WORLD CHAMPION".*

LEFT: *This 1992 Suzuki DR650 is typical of larger Japanese off-road bikes: all modern conveniences, including an electric start, and styling and tyres that are aimed as much at the on-road market as at the off-road market. Shrouded disks and wire-spoked wheels show genuine off-road potential, though.*

If you do this, you can reach places that would be totally inaccessible to anyone but the most dedicated hiker, and (if your tastes lie that way) you can picnic in the most extraordinary surroundings; beside crystal pools where the only sounds are the occasional plash of water, the soughing of the wind in the trees, and the quiet click and ping of cooling metal.

You can ride along roads that were old when the Romans came to Britain, and which have never been surfaced; if you look closely at your Ordnance Survey maps you will see the designation "Road Used as a Public Path." Known to their friends as RUPPs, these are open to all vehicular traffic; and you can see an England which is extraordinarily unchanged by the Industrial Revolution.

You can traverse forests; you can explore roads that are used only by loggers or by inspectors of dams; you can go to places you might not have believed existed. You are, however, running some very considerable risks.

The first is to your own health and safety. If you get it wrong, and fall off badly enough to hurt yourself, you may be unable to get back for help; in which case you can quite easily die. Motorcyclists are by their very nature risk-takers, but this is overdoing things! It is all but essential, if you want to try this sort of wilderness or semi-wilderness riding, to adopt some sort of "buddy system" and ride with *at least* one friend on his or her own, separate motorcycle. If this is not possible, you can increase your chances of being found by telling people *exactly* where you are going, and asking them to come looking for you if you do not return in a given time.

Quite apart from your own life and limb, you have to consider the health of the motorcycle. If you cannot perform a basic diagnostic sequence on your motorcycle, and remedy simple faults, you should not be venturing into places where you cannot find a mechanic. Carry simple tools, and make sure you are able to check spark, fuel, plugs, etc. and to carry out simple repairs.

Carry a puncture-repair outfit, too. Repairing a puncture may not be much fun, but it beats being stuck twenty miles from nowhere with only an hour and a half of daylight left.

And thirdly, regardless of your well-being or the motorcycle's, you have a duty to consider what you are doing for the image of motorcycling at large. There are countless riders who are totally indifferent to what you do to your own miserable hide or to your own miserable motorcycle, but if by your antics you alienate the general public, thereby leading to unnecessary restrictions on riders who do know how to behave, these same people who are so totally indifferent to your existence would cheerfully save you the trouble of hurting yourself in an accident. The larger and more aggressive among them might even be willing to arrange a fork-stanchion as a bow tie. Others might prefer to lead you to a babbling brook, then hold your head under it and count to a hundred and one.

The rules are simple: keep quiet, and don't tear the place up. A certain amount of noise is inevitable from any mechanically-propelled vehicle, but pulling out the baffles to make more noise is the sort of thing you would expect from a brain-dead sixteen-year-old. Riding as quietly as you can, on a bike that is as quiet as possible, will alienate the minimum number of people. As for tearing the place up, if you are riding properly you will leave almost no trace of your passing.

Or maybe there is even a fifth style. It's super-specialized, and at the time of writing it was by no means certain that the machine you need to pursue it will continue to be available. It is serious off-roading with an outfit that has sidecar drive.

BELOW: *The Honda works trials bike shows that the big Japanese companies are not going to let the small,* *specialist firms have things all their own way: this is a serious competitive motorcycle.*

The origin of this remarkable device seems to lie in the Second World War, when the *Wehrmacht* needed a "go-anywhere" vehicle. They had the Volkswagen-based *Kubelwagen* and even the amphibious *Schwimmkubel*, it was true. They also had various types of half-track, including the *Kettenrad*. But what they didn't have was an equivalent to the Jeep; a cheap, almost disposable off-road vehicle that could be driven just about anywhere.

What they did, therefore, was to take the time-honoured and well-tested BMW-style flat twin, and add a sidecar; a traditional form of military transport which could trace its lineage back to World War One. Then, in order to improve the off-road capability of what was essentially an awkward and ill-balanced machine with only one of its three wheels driven, they added a power take off which allowed the sidecar wheel to be driven.

With the defeat of Germany, that might well have been that. But the wily Russians, with a vast country served for the most part by appalling roads, decided to make their own version of the sidecar-drive BMW.

The result, which was still available new at the time of writing, was the most unbelievable, exhilarating, indestructible, ill-thought-out off-road vehicle of all time; and one which, furthermore, would go almost anywhere.

Unlike the Jeep, which could be driven by any fool who could sit in the driving seat, the sidecar-drive Ural (and its German predecessor) required not only maniacal bravery, but also extraordinary skill and preferably three arms; the most successful teams allegedly divided responsibilities for gear changing, with the rider doing most of the work and the sidecar passenger lending a hand on the tricky bits.

With only about 34 bhp, the sidecar-drive Ural is not a spectacular roadburner, but in a vehicle that weighs only about 600 lb, and where the rider and passenger(s) can engage in all kinds of creative weight transfer techniques to keep the vehicle upright, the overall result can only be described as incredible. Whether crabbing up the side of a sand-dune, or sliding down the side of a quarry where the laws of gravity would seem to rule out anything but a straight drop, this is one of life's most memorable vehicles. Sure, there are ordinary sidecar dirt bikes, but this thing is the experience of a lifetime.

ABOVE: "comings-together" are not unusual on the dirt track but, perhaps suprisingly, serious injuries are rare. Here, Neilsen and Muller collide against a backdrop of blue smoke and a rather unexpected pedestrian crossing the track. The other two riders exhibit the typical foot-dragging stance of the dirt-track rider: even steel-shod boots wear rapidly.

RIGHT: For some reason grass-track racing is regarded as a sport suitable for the young; perhaps because they are foolhardy and their bones mend easily. The best schoolboy riders – this is Jeremy Luckham in 1989 – are not foolhardy at all, they are very, very good riders indeed. "Grass track" is, however, something of a euphemism.

RIGHT: *Gaylon Mosier flies high in a typically dramatic Don Morley shot. A skilled rider like Mosier, who has reconnoitred the course, can jump for impressive distances and come down safely. The danger comes when a less skilled rider tries it, especially when they "yump" over hillocks and sand dunes without knowing what is on the other side. More than one rider has broken his neck that way, finishing his riding career for all time and making rather a mess of his life in the process.*

BELOW: *Desert or sand-dune racing is immense fun, but a great deal more difficult than it looks: the directional stability of a motorcycle in soft sand is very poor, and the sand which seems so soft when you are riding over it is distressingly hard when you fall off and land on it. Also, like most forms of off-road racing, you have to be careful where you do it: riding in the wrong place is not only inconsiderate, but can also lead to ever-wider bans on off-road riding.*

LEFT: *The ISDE (International Six Days' Event, formerly International Six Days' Trial) is closer than most races to "real world" conditions: riders have to repair breakdowns, mend punctures (as Holger Herbertz is doing here in the 1983 event), and compromise on tyres. In many races, by contrast, tyres, gear ratios, engines and even whole bikes are swapped for specific stages.*

BELOW: *Vintage moto-cross meets like the one photographed here always have an air of camaraderie about them. If you are trying to cross difficult terrain on a motorcycle that is well over a quarter of a century old, you are probably doing it for love rather than money: this is one of the increasingly rare forms of sport where it really is more important to play the game than to win.*

ABOVE: *Climbing rock-faces is one thing that trials riders are known for. Splashing dramatically through streams is another. Then you try combining the two, and riding up through waterfalls…. This hero/ lunatic/sportsman is another ISDE contestant, showing people what can be done by a good enough rider. At this level, the big problem lies in finding motorcycles that are up to the demands of the riders.*

RIGHT: *Juhani Larrsonen demonstrates in the 1983 ISDE that the Finns can be every bit as unstoppable on two wheels as they are on four. He is riding on a poor surface in marginal light, and still managing to go alarmingly quickly. Of course, he will have reconnoitred the track carefully first, and he has enormous experience: lesser riders should take to heart Batman's warning, "Kids, do not try this at home."*

FACING PAGE: *"Flat track" racing remains popular (and highly skilled) in the USA because it reflects the skills that many young Americans hone in a large, sparsely-populated country where there is plenty of opportunity for practising off-road riding in adverse conditions. Perhaps curiously, their greatest rivals in this (and in the similar sport of ice-racing) are often East Europeans.*

RIGHT AND BELOW: *"Super-X" is a highly contrived spectator sport derived from "real" off-road riding. Life is not significantly easier for the riders, but it is much easier for "couch potato" spectators: no walking across awkward terrain, no risk of getting showered with mud or water, and plenty of vendors selling snacks and drinks. This is at Anaheim, also the home of Disneyland.*

Be honest: would you be totally confident about walking up the slope that Steffan Merriman is climbing on the left? A slope like this looks steep in a photograph: from the seat of the rider's Aprilia it looks (and sometimes feels) like a vertical cliff face. The Scottish Six Days', where this was shot in 1991, is very much an event for serious riders.

In the picture above, there is a sudden jolt when you realize that Eric Brandauer of Austria is not just "yumping" in mid air: his rear wheel is in contact with a very substantial portion of the scenery.

BELOW: *Some idea of the popularity of competitive off-road riding can be gained from this picture of the* parc ferme, *where the bikes are impounded after scrutineering in order to make sure that their riders do not make unapproved modifications. Reputedly, when the ISDE was hotly contested by unscrupulous teams from the former Eastern Bloc, there were all kinds of ruses, including engine-cases stamped with identical numbers but filled with very different machinery; support teams who were rumored to hide in remote dells to give riders mechanical assistance; and even whole duplicate bikes. Some of these stories may be true, but others are probably just "sour grapes" from the losers.*

LEFT AND FACING PAGE: *It is disputable whether the spectator can see more at events like the 1990 World Trials Championship (Jordi Tarres on his Beta is seen on the left) or at lesser events. Even riders like Eddy Lejeune (right) often ride at events where access is surprisingly good, and where spectators can watch the most extraordinary feats from remarkably close up. The low rear tyre pressure and the "over-the-bars" forward stance enable Eddy to ride his Honda up a slope which most people would tackle on their hands and knees. Low tyre pressures – as low as 0,3 bar (5 psi) – are one secret of getting maximum possible grip, but on faster sections of the course, higher pressures are required. Knowing where to compromise is an essential skill.*

LEFT: *This 1991 Aprilia Climber illustrates how the big manufacturers are sometimes humbled by names which are hardly known outside the competitive world of dirt-bike riding: Aprilia and Beta are just two of the better-known names. The requirements for climbing are actually different from those required for traversing bad flat terrain: you need a longer swinging arm, and much greater suspension movement at the rear than at the front.*

FACING PAGE: *just when you think you've seen it all... At the 1991 Scottish Six Days' Trial, pedestrians gingerly pick their way across ankle-breaking boulders as a lone rider (M. Martin) actually* persuades a motorcycle to traverse the same terrain. Remember, if he puts one foot down (a "dab") he will lose points: he must cross "feet up."

ABOVE: *All Quiet on the Western Front. Even the most heroic (crazy?) sidecar pilots, like Larry Baker, get bogged down sometimes. When they do, the only possibility is human muscle power, to* drag the outfit out of the thick, clinging mud and get it back onto a firm enough surface to try and start all over again. And people do this for fun?

DIRT

BELOW AND RIGHT: *Ice racing is seriously weird! The wheels are shod with massively spiked tyres, and the rider's right leg is steel-shod and protected with heavy leather leggings. The bikes, like the Jawa below, are essentially dirt-track machines with extended mudguards to provide some protection from the wheels in the event of a spill. Those ferocious spikes provide extraordinary grip, however, and allow the riders* to corner at lean angles which frankly defy belief: Milan Spinka, of the former USSR, demonstrates how it is done in the picture on the right. To a very large extent, ice-racing is dominated by East European and Scandinavian riders, though there are some from the United States and even England.

FACING PAGE: *Erik Stenlund of Sweden demonstrates the near-horizontal style of riding which has to be mastered by serious ice racers. This picture also illustrates why the left leg and foot are protected as they are: ice races are always run counter-clockwise, like traditional flat-track races, and for much of the race the leg is actually sliding on the ice. The traditional material for protecting the leg is thick rawhide, and even in an era of plastic "body armour" and high-tech Kevlar-reinforced leathers, there are still few materials which offer any significant advantages. This is the sort of riding position that most of us experience only in nightmares – or after we have lost control!*

The sight of an ice-racing bike pulling a wheelie is rather like the sight of a Tyrannosaurus Rex looking for dinner: it's impressive, but you don't want to be too close when it happens. ABOVE: Svoboda and Stanislav of the former USSR pull some crowd-pleasing stunts and (more or less) amiably dare each other to do anything even more spectacular. Both are mounted on Czech-built Jawa singles, widely

acknowledged as the definitive motorcycle for this rather specialized form of racing. On the left, the awesome spikes and the "safety-fence" front mudguard can be seen clearly: you need to be a brave man just to go close to one of these monsters, let alone ride one!

Ice racing is a popular spectator sport in those countries where it exists, but it does not translate very well

to television. It is still dramatic, but nothing can capture the full assault on the senses that is ice racing at its best: bright, warm sun on a bitterly cold day, the scream and roar of the engines, the ice-chips flung into the air, the sharp, clear smell of burning oil.

3
TOURING

If racing is a whirlwind romance with a beautiful but temperamental exotic dancer, touring is a good marriage with a great spouse: a long-term partnership with its share of setbacks and irritations, but always with a deeper and deeper understanding of your partner, bejewelled with unexpected pleasures and old, familiar delights.

By and large – barring those who only want to race, or who only want to pose for the admiration of others – there are two kinds of motorcyclists: those who want to go touring, and those who want to go touring again. The first time you venture more than a few miles from home on a two-wheeler, you get a glimpse of touring, of life in the here-and-now in a new environment. Because you are more alert, you notice things more; and because you notice things more, you feel more alive. Because you feel more alive, you want to prolong the experience.

And the wonderful thing is that you can. Touring is easy. Sure, there are mistakes you can make, things you can forget, times you will be cold and wet and miserable. But there are countless more ways of doing things right.

Some people do it all on the cheap: tents, pressure stoves, washing in the stream. Others spend thousands on escorted tours, where even the bikes are hired and where every room, every meal, is booked in advance, and the luggage is carried in an escort van. Some ride full-dress behemoths, six-cylinder Honda Goldwings and Suzuki Cavalcades and Yamaha Ventures, maybe even with trailers. Others ride tiny motorcycles: Honda 90s, even mopeds. And the vast majority are somewhere in the middle.

The great thing about touring – like any sort of motorcycling – is that no-one can tell you how to do it. As Kipling wrote, "There are nine and sixty ways of constructing tribal lays, And–every–single–one–of–them–is–right!"

The Great American Tour really requires the Great American Tourer, an enormous motorcycle set up like a rolling gin-palace. Huge "King and Queen" seats coddle the rump; a sound system

Do It Your Way: touring is just as much fun whether your tastes run to camping in Wales (left) or to touring Austria and staying in hotels (top). The only difficulty lies in simultaneously marshalling enough time and enough money: the agony and the ecstasy come automatically.

With an automobile, the scenery is something outside, something separate – even if you are driving a convertible. But with a motorcycle you are much more a part of the world around you. Not only can you feel the sun and the wind on your face, and breathe the constantly-changing odours all around you: more important still, you do not see everything through the picture-frame of a windshield, or have the road's irregularities concealed from you by overly supple suspension. There is more incentive to stop, to get off, to explore, as at Hanging Rock State Park in North Carolina (facing page). Even a big, heavy motorcycle will get you to places where a car would never go, while an off-road bike like the 250cc and 500cc Hondas (left) can carry a surprising load but can become tiring and tedious on long rides on the highway.

helps while away the time as you cross immense landscapes where the scenery changes but slowly as the hundreds of miles roll up on the odometer. Speeds are low; although the dreaded "double nickel" 55 mph speed limit (just under 90 kph) has now yielded to 65 mph (about 105 kph) on the interstates, many touring motorcyclists still ride incredibly slowly by European standards. This is because of massive fairings (and sometimes trailers) that would be extremely dangerous at anything much more than a mile a minute, and a sit-up-and-beg riding position which would be extremely tiring at high speeds. There are Americans who will tell you in all seriousness that it is impossible for a "normal" rider to control any motorcycle at 80 mph (130 kph) or above.

Distances boggle the European imagination. You could ride from London to Istanbul, and you would still not have ridden the equivalent of New York to Los Angeles. The ride from Los Angeles to San Francisco is 400 miles, and there is still plenty of California south of the City of the Angels and plenty more north of the City of St. Francis. And if you want to go any distance, the Interstates seem to go on forever: long, long roads with few curves, where everyone is on autopilot and you could fall asleep on a motorcycle, let alone driving a car.

On the back roads, there is good news and there is bad news. First the bad news. Nowhere in the world are motorcyclists so feared and so hated, by so many people, as in the United States. Restaurants and bars may refuse to serve you; motels may suddenly find that there are no vacancies, even though there are no cars in the parking lot. But the good news is that if they will serve you – and more will than won't – it's the cheapest, easiest country in the world in which to go motorcycle touring.

Snapshot: the Far Western Tavern in Guadalupe, California. Without really knowing what you are getting into, you order the most expensive item on the menu, the 20-ounce (570 gm) fillet steak. The waitress in blue jeans takes your order, goes through the litany of options. The bus-boy brings the appetizer tray: peppers and spring onions and celery and two more kinds of peppers and carrots and olives. Then comes the soup, and then the salad, and finally the steak, an enormous slab of meat cooked on an oak-pit barbecue, served with a baked potato, Santa Maria style barbecued beans, and a salsa of tomato, onion, chili peppers and cilantro. There is garlic bread on the side. You'd better be hungry. The meat is lean, tender, barely warm on the inside, superbly cooked on the outside – the carnivore's dream of a rare steak. The bill is ridiculously low: for this price, you would

ABOVE: *"Colorado's Freedom Ride 1989" by Mike Lichter. A few states still allow motorcyclists to ride without helmets, but the number falls annually: California made helmets compulsory in 1992. Most motorcyclists, even if they normally wear helmets, would go along with the Motorcycle Action Group slogan: "Helmets yes, compulsion no." Some clubs organize protest rides without helmets.*

RIGHT: *Touring is as much about where you stop as about where you ride; Stove Pipe Wells is in Death Valley. The Harley may look righteous, but it shows how not to load a bike for touring: the loads are high and outside the wheelbase, where they will have the maximum adverse effect on handling. Anyone crossing Death Valley should of course carry tools and water.*

consider yourself lucky to get a good Indian meal in England, a good Algerian meal in France, a good Yugoslav meal in Germany. And this is an expensive meal by the standards of most Americans.

Snapshot: a small motel in Jackson, Georgia. In the town square, there is the usual memorial TO OUR CONFEDERATE DEAD. The owner of the motel shows you a room; basic, but clean, with its own bathroom and air conditioner. You take it. It costs less than a comparable room would cost in the motel-owner's native India. As the trip progresses, you learn that if you want a good, cheap motel, you sniff for the aroma of curry cooking in the owner's quarters before you even bother to ask the price or see the room.

Snapshot: sitting on a sun-warmed rock in Yosemite, beside a little lake ten thousand feet above sea level. You spread the picnic on the rock: the Mexican cheese, the Pennsylvania Dutch pretzels, the Texan pickled okra, the Wisconsin butter, the pumpernickel imported from Germany. Gingerly you unwire the cage from the Californian "champagne": not only is it shaken up from the ride, but you are unsure how much extra force the cork will have at that altitude. You ease it a fraction of an inch from the neck; it bursts free and arcs two-thirds of the way across the lake.

Snapshot: you stop to fill the bike. The price is quoted in a bizarre unit, the American gallon, which is neither metric (it's just over 3.6 litres) nor Imperial (it's four-fifths the size of a "real" gallon). But you can fill the tank for about one-third as much as it would cost you anywhere in Europe.

Snapshot: poring over a map in the Shenandoah Valley (map-making is one of the arts the American colonists lost after they separated from the Mother Country). Slowly, you work out that the Yankee forces were camped *here*, so the Confederate forces must have taken *this* road and *this* path, and crossed Cedar Creek *here*. It's a far cry from the Disneyland that Gettysburg has

ABOVE: *For some people, the great attraction of touring is that they are on their own, but others prefer to ride in groups. It's all a matter of personal preference.*

ABOVE: *Many motorcyclists maintain that the ideal number of people on a tour is two: one rider, one pillion.*

TOURING

RIGHT: *You can leave the bike right outside the gates to the Taj Mahal; parking in India is lightly controlled at most, and you can leave a motorcycle almost anywhere. Nor is theft much of a problem: if you want to leave the bike unlocked and fully laden, hire a guard for ten or twenty rupees.*

BELOW: *The Sturgis Motorcycle Classic is a pilgrimage for Harley riders; literally thousands of riders converge on this small town in the middle of nowhere, which is where the riders below are heading. For a few days every year Sturgis is as important to Harley riders as Milwaukee.*

become, and it brings home to you the realities of what true Southerners still call the War of Northern Aggression.

Snapshots: desert roads arrow-straight to the horizon; the smell of pines on the Blue Ridge Highway; the state capitol at Raleigh, North Carolina, with its perfectly-proportioned interior, a cool and shady respite from a humid Southern summer. The houses at Marblehead in New England, conspicuous consumption hiding behind a gloss of restraint. The cannon lathe on the green in Selma, Alabama. The ersatz shoot-'em-up towns in the Wild West; the incredible colours of the Painted Desert in Arizona, the Pennsylvania roadside diners like something out of the Great Depression. Everywhere, the flag flying; it's not a special holiday, Americans just like to fly their flag.

For an American, the great thing about touring America is that it is there. To a foreigner, the attraction is much the same. How can you not see America for yourself?

To anyone brought up in the English-speaking world, though, motorcycle touring in continental Europe is a revelation. Motorcyclists are treated as human beings. Motorcycles can be parked on the pavement. No-one bats an eyelid when you walk into a hotel or a restaurant carrying a crash-helmet.

Speed limits are high, and are not always too rigorously enforced: the 130 kph limit (81 mph) on French *péage* (toll) *autoroutes* is effectively a license to do anything up to about 150 kph (93 mph), and even the 110 kph (68 mph) limit on non-toll *autoroutes* is routinely interpreted to mean something in the 120-130 kph range (75-80 mph). In Germany, there are no speed limits at all on much of the autobahn network, and you can cruise at whatever speed your motorcycle, your nerves and your stamina can sustain.

Distances are (comparatively) short. From Paris to the Mediterranean coast is only about 400 miles (650 km) as the crow flies, and on the *péage* roads that's less than five hours riding. Luxembourg is maybe two hours from Köln (Cologne), three hours from Paris or Amsterdam, an easy day's ride from Berlin or Venice or Prague. The whole continent beckons.

Because of this, and because there are still people in Europe who regard a motorcycle as serious transport instead of as a toy, you meet all sorts of people on all sorts of motorcycles all over Europe, from those who regard a day wasted when they do not cover 600 miles (1000 km) to those who feel that they are missing the scenery and the ambiance if they exceed a couple of hundred miles (320 km) in a day. You see them hurtling down the autobahn at 140 mph (225 kph), and you see them pottering along the back roads, or riding through mediaeval towns and villages, as slowly as their bikes will carry them in first gear. You see them on Italian sports-bikes with rock-hard suspensions and all their luggage in a briefcase strapped to the back of the seat; you see them on elderly Matchlesses bulging with luggage tied in place with codline, kettles and cooking pots tied to the bedroll beside the tent.

Snapshot: the far north of Portugal, the part called Trás-os-Montes ("Beyond the Mountains"). This is as far from the beach-and-tourists Portugal as you can imagine. Pine forests fall to the sides of high lakes. The roads twist and wind through the mountains; you know you will be lucky to average even 30 mph (50 kph) – but you don't care, because the air is clear and perfect and the weather is clear and perfect and as soon as you find the right spot you are going to sit down to a picnic of good Portuguese bread and cheese, olives and *vinho verde*, the light wine they call "green" because it is drunk young. You are heading for a *pousada*, a country inn which you know will be beautifully located in stunning scenery, with a first-class restaurant attached. How do you know? Because they are *all* like that.

Snapshot: you have been riding all day, and the weather is just coming on to rain. You decide to investigate the next town that

ABOVE: *Vernal Falls in Yosemite National Park: one* *of America's most stunning touring destinations.*

looks half-way presentable. You see the sign; 18 km. You follow the road. Suddenly, you are in a maze of half-timbered buildings, the lights just coming on as the autumn day ends. You ride straight past the hotel, make a series of awkward turns to get back. You summon all your German: "Haben sie ein doppelzimmer mit bad, bitte?" The hotelier, a fat, almost cartoon German, nods a broad *Ja*. You check the room; it really is a *bad*, a bath, not a *dusche*, a shower. Your very bones begin to relax as you think of a long, hot soak and an inch of Asbach Uralt brandy in the tooth-glass. You know you will sleep very well tonight.

Snapshot: you wake early, because you go to bed early and leave the curtains open so that you will be woken by the sun. From your hotel room you can see the Alps beckoning, seemingly only a few kilometres away in the crystalline air though you know they must be a couple of hours' ride. All through that day, you ride through the Alps, crossing borders a dozen times, weaving in and out of Austria and Switzerland and Bavaria. It is like riding through a picture postcard: cows with clonking cow-bells, peaks reflected in lakes, deep-green grass looking as smooth and perfect as a bowling green. You use six rolls of film, trying to capture the beauty; years later, those pictures will transport you back to that perfect day instantly, the day you did not even stop for lunch because you were too hungry for more sights, more beauty.

Snapshot: a winding, narrow, gravel-surfaced road snakes up to a castle on a hill-top. There is a smell of dust in your nostrils. You ride up slowly in first gear; traction is not all it might be, and you wonder what it will be like coming down. As you rise higher, the twentieth century drops away: no more power lines, no more telephone lines. You begin to fantasize about being caught in a time-warp. Will they sell petrol in cans? Or have you left the twentieth century altogether? How will the Spanish Inquisition react to motorcycles?

Snapshot: a summer morning. You can see the village ahead of you as you smell the new-cut hay. You slow, then pull out to overtake a tractor pulling a load of manure; no mistaking that smell. As you enter the village, the first shop you pass is the bakery, the rich odour of baking and fresh-baked bread: you stop to buy fresh croissants, a *pain chocolat* for breakfast. On the high street each shop announces its business with a different smell: coffee roasting at the grocer's, the smell of metal and oil at the

ABOVE: *Even when confronted with the glory of the Painted Desert, many drivers never get out of their cars. Can you believe that?*

RIGHT: *"Waal," says the cowboy at the end of the movie, "I guess I'll just keep headin' west – ridin' on into the sunset ...."*

garage, an elusive whiff of chocolate as you pass the confectioners. You feel almost as if you could ride blindfold, and every breath is as fresh as the moment.

Snapshots: cruising at 110-115 mph (180 kph) in Germany, and there are *still* Porsches passing you like you are standing still. The Champs Elysees as the lights come on, the Arc de Triomphe a brilliant gold against the deepening blue of the sky. Eleven miles of cobbled country road in Portugal. Bicyclists weaving around you in Amsterdam. Your beat-up touring bike parked dusty and travel-stained at Cannes, among the immaculate Paris-Dakar replicas and state-of-the-art sports bikes – and see who gets the attention!

In Europe, you can go "touring" in a day, and you can cross half a dozen countries in a week-end. History lies thicker than the leaves of the forest, but you are also exploring the future: a Europe increasingly without borders, increasingly cosmopolitan, increasingly powerful and important.

But maybe even Europe isn't the ultimate touring experience. Consider ... India.

India is uniquely India, but it is also the England of several decades ago: the quaint grammatical constructions, the punctilious politeness, the appalling bureaucracy, the prices. There is a sense of the exotic, weirdly interwoven with a sense of *déjà vu*.

The only bike to tour on, of course, is the India Enfield Bullet, as described in Chapter 2. Available both as a 350 and a 500, the 500 offers only a few more horsepower (22 bhp instead of 17 bhp), but it offers unbelievable torque and flexibility. The frame is virtually indestructible: with a dry weight of 168 Kg (370 lb.) it offers a 250 Kg (550 lb.) payload!

On this time-machine you can trundle happily all over India, secure in the knowledge that anything which goes wrong can be replaced in the bazaar for a few rupees; mechanics everywhere know how this thing works, and the parts cost very little indeed. You have to readjust your whole world-picture to take care of your schedules, though, and you will be doing well if you can average the same sort of speeds in kilometres per hour that you would expect to achieve in Europe in miles per hour. In other words, if you normally reckon on averaging 40-50 mph (65-80 kph) on European non-motorway roads, and covering 300 miles (500 km) on an average day, reckon instead on 40-50 kph (25-30 mph) and 300 km (185 miles).

Snapshot: swinging up the hill road to Udaghamandalam (or Ootacamund, or Ooty – all three variants appear on the signposts). In third gear, despite the load and the incline, the engine pulls smoothly with an incredible exhaust note; every firing stroke can be heard. Monkeys scatter out of the road as you change down into second for a particularly tight hairpin, then sit watching you as you continue to climb. If their ears were attuned to motorcycles they would hear the engine note return to the slow beat as you successfully navigate the bend, and keep on climbing.

Snapshot: in the bazaar, you leave the bike to be serviced. Oil change; general lubrication and adjustment; and there's a wire frayed on the clutch cable, so you ask them to replace it while they are at it. Small boys are despatched to fetch the necessary parts, and to bring cold drinks, a Thums Up or a Campa Cola. You sit and wait for a while, but it becomes clear that things are going to take longer than expected. Knowing that the machine and your luggage are in good hands, you wander off into the bazaar. It is a sensory kaleidoscope: flowers, fruit, vegetables, spices, less pleasant odours. A pig runs by, surprisingly briskly; it is being chased by a small boy with a stick. A swineherd's son? A stallholder's son? A freelance pig-chaser, harrying the hapless swine because it is the nature of small boys to chase things? Who can tell? When at last you return to pick up the bike, two rolls of film later, they tell you that they have also replaced the clutch thrust bearing; the old one, looking somewhat the worse for wear, is produced for your inspection. But the bill is still well under a hundred rupees, rather less than £4 or maybe $6.

Snapshot: breakfast on the beach in Goa. You pop the cork of a bottle of Marquis de Pompadour Indian Champagne into the Arabian Sea, sheltering from the sun in the lee of a beached

BELOW: *"I've got a feeling we're not in Kansas any more." An unusually uncrowded Tokyo street gives an erroneous impression of Japan, where the city streets* are pure murder. Out in the open country speed limits are low, but you get to see the "real" Japan that many people think has vanished.

BELOW: *At the end of the day …. It's a beautiful image, and a classic dream, but would you really want to go touring on a bike with the rear wheel off a dump truck and the front wheel off a* bicycle? An anti-Harley activist might add that the motor came out of a cement-mixer. But fortunately motorcyclists rarely come to blows over their choices of bikes.

fishing-boat. As you eat your unconventional repast of raw cashews, fresh fruit and champagne, a little girl of eight or ten comes by selling jewellery. You buy a pair or earrings for your wife. Later, you will ride on the hard-packed sand of the foreshore: a dozen miles, almost twenty kilometres, of perfect tropical beach.

Snapshot: somewhere in the hills on the Mysore-Bangalore road, they filmed *A Passage to India*. You decide to investigate the huge, rocky outcrops more closely. The road goes from being surfaced to being unsurfaced, then from a road to a two-rutter. The two-rutter passes through a scrubby village, becomes a one-rutter footpath, then peters out in dried-up paddy fields. Two villagers ask what you were looking for; did you know that this was where they filmed *A Passage to India*. Yes, you did. But did you know that the temple they built is just over there, no distance? You did not. You prepare to walk with them, but they explain no, there is a very good road, just across this field, built for the film crew. You must bring your motorcycle. With some trepidation, you follow. They are right; it is not far, only half a mile. But half a mile over dried-up rice-paddies is a surprisingly long way on a motorcycle.

Snapshots: a long, clear road like something in the west of America, and 110 kph (68 mph) on the clock: it feels like 110 mph (175 kph). Riding past a crocodile farm with a wonderfully graphic "No Swimming" sign alongside. Indian traffic: an endless snarl-up, catch-as-catch-can, people riding and driving in both directions on both sides of the centre divider, but (miraculously) no-one getting hurt. Dust. The blessed cool of a 50 kph breeze on a day too hot to stand still. Waterfalls cascading down the sides of hills, people bathing and washing at the bottom. Tea-gardens, cardamom-fields, the smell of eucalyptus-oil stills. Wonderful meals in unknown hotels and restaurants. A bottle of "Knock-Out" beer in Shimoga; a rum-tasting session (Old Monk, Carib, Black Bull and a couple of others) in Margao. Fishermen setting out in dug-out canoes in impossibly beautiful dawns.

Back at home, the motorcycle magazines just do not seem the same. THE MOST BEAUTIFUL RIDE OF YOUR LIFE – GUARANTEED, they promise. There are escorted tours of the Alps, of Australia, of the Alaskan highway. But you have seen things more beautiful than they can imagine, and you dream of sights yet more beautiful, yet more exotic. One day the Chinese empire will fall, and when it does there is a perfectly good trade route between Kalimpong and Lhasa. Greedily you work out the itinerary: Rangli, Nathang, across the Jelep-la pass into Tibet at about 10,500 feet (3175 metres). Yatung, Geling, Chumbi. After Phari Dzong it's a road again, not just a camel track – but Phari Dzong is at 14,300 feet, almost 4,400 metres.

All right, that's a bit exotic. But there were all those hilltop castles you never got to explore last time you were in Portugal. There are those boulder-strewn landscapes in the Alps that you passed through fairly smartly because it was February and you were afraid of the snows. There are all those gold-country towns in California that are off Highway 49; the ones that aren't so heavily visited by tourists, but which (from the one or two that you have seen) appear to be even more intriguing.

Then there are the places you have never been, but always wondered about: Ireland, maybe, or the Peloponnese. And the places you may have been in a car, but not on a motorcycle: heading inland from Mazatlan to Durango, the tiny, history-soaked islands of Malta and Gozo, crossroads of the known world for five thousand years. On a motorcycle, everything you experience will be more real, more immediate, more memorable.

LEFT: *Do Not Try This At Home. Riding a motorcycle on the hard-packed sand of the foreshore is a motorcyclist's dream, but make sure that you do not have to cross loose sand en route if you are riding something like this Goldwing Interstate. If you bog it down, you are going to need a lot of strong-arm assistance to dig it out again; not for nothing is the Goldwing nicknamed the Leadwing. Having said all that, it is amazing where you can persuade even a monster bike like this to go, with the right combination of experience, foolhardiness and damn-the-torpedoes bravado.*

Motorways, autobahns, autoroutes and autostrade are fine for getting from A to B fast, but is that what motorcycling necessarily has to be about? The back roads are where you really get to learn about a country, and where you have a chance to think about Life, the Universe and Everything. The sights, the sounds, the smells – everything comes together. You don't need a state-of-the-art bike, or a lot of money – just a sunny day and a little fuel.

BELOW: *The traditionalist's machine: the lordly BMW 100 with its "retro" styling, simple but solid.*

ABOVE: *Rallies exist to cater for all tastes, from well-padded, middle-aged couples on luxo-tourers to those who wear their heads backwards. The fire is unusually impressive, but the beer is universal.*

ABOVE: *Bikes as far as the eye can see at the Dutch TT. Even those riders who prefer to be alone will recognize the swelling of the spirit, the joyfulness of the heart, which comes from being in the company of hundreds or even thousands of other riders. Motorcycling is inherently an emotional experience, and there is some sort of pooling of emotion which creates a new feeling, something which transcends everyday life and even everyday motorcycling.*

RIGHT: *Not all highs are good highs: night is falling fast, rain is falling faster, and there's a Mercedes 16-wheeler on your tail on a slick road. You haven't booked a room for the night, but you want a bath, a real bath with lots of hot water. How long are you going to hold out before you accept a room with a shower? Ah, well, never mind: tomorrow is another day, and besides, it's still better than being at work.*

FACING PAGE: *Well, yes, I know I said you can tour on anything; but this is ridiculous …. Seriously, it has its possibilities: drive somewhere nice, get the bikes out of the back of the car, and use them for exploring. Then, at the end of the day, put them back in the car, drive to the hotel and rest in comfort. Hey, you're beginning to persuade me already. After all, not every tour has to be an Iron Butt endurance special. And maybe, once they've finished playing with their executive toys, even yuppies can learn how to ride real motorcycles instead of driving hot hatchbacks. Now, bite your lip and say after me, "All motorcyclists are brothers. All motorcyclists are brothers. All motorcyclists …."*

ABOVE: *Forget Sturgis: this is where real motorcyclists go on their honeymoon – the   Island, for TT week.*

You don't even need to say which Island, because there is only one Island: the Isle of Man, where they hold the Tourist Trophy races in June every year. You don't need to say which TT, either: this is **the** *TT, the last great round-the-houses race.*

LEFT: *The boarding houses at Douglas recall the days when the British took their seaside holidays seriously. Today, business is slack – except during the magic of TT week, when serious riders from all over the world converge to* watch the racing and to try the track themselves, on Mad Sunday.

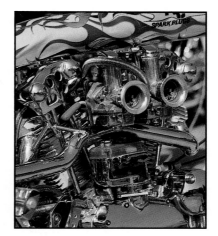

4
CUSTOM

As soon as you do anything that alters your machine from its factory specification, you have a custom bike. It may be something as modest as adding luggage, or it may be as radical as rebuilding the engine, reversing the heads, slotting it into a hardtail frame and adding eighteen-inch-over forks topped off with "ape-hanger" bars.

The classic bike to "customize" is of course the Harley-Davidson, but this is no doubt due in part to the fact that for so many years the basic Harley design was so unutterably awful that the only way to turn it into anything that was worth having was to customize it. Eventually the factory cottoned on to this, and the (somewhat oxymoronic) "Factory Custom" was born, a machine which used the basic Harley building-blocks and did to them what owners had been doing for many years – whether what the owners did made any sense or not.

Incomparably the loveliest Harley "Factory Custom" was one of the earliest, the XLCR, which was first shown as a styling exercise in 1974 and then put into production in 1977. Reputedly, it was also Willie G. Davidson's favourite Harley ever, and assuredly it was a commercial flop: very few of these delightful machines were ever built. But in order to understand the XLCR you have to go back to the 1950s and the "Cafe Racers" that were ridden (and built) by England's "Ton-Up Boys" or "Rockers."

In the England of those days there were no motorways. There were a few roads which might just about be considered today to be of motorway standard, i.e. long, straight dual carriageways (what the Americans call "divided roads") with central dividers and two lanes in either direction, but they were few and far between. The vast majority of main roads, called "A" Roads in the parlance of the day, were winding and consisted for the most part of two lanes, though there were also stretches of "three-lane killer," where the centre lane was used for overtaking in both directions. Even the best roads, which would consist of a mixture of dual-carriageway, four-lane without a centre divider, three-

The Harley (left) is a classic, nicely-executed and none-too-radical chop: if it were not for the paint job, it would probably attract no attention at all. Compared with the utterly over-the-top Arlen Ness Accell (top) it barely departs from stock; but it's a lot easier to ride.

CUSTOM

BELOW: *Harleys are arguably the only bikes that can really take gold plating: they are so far over the top already that selective gilding merely serves to emphasize the neo-medieval engine. The SU* carb *interferes with the rider's knee, and the tank holds only a few pints of fuel, but this is clearly a machine where form takes precedence over function.*

lane killer and plain two-lane, would periodically be funnelled through villages which had been laid out centuries before, with extremely narrow roads, plenty of side-turnings, and an apparent incomprehension of the concept of roads that went in straight lines.

There were also no speed limits on the open road.

This led to a demand for motorcycles with nimble handling, to cope with all the twists and turns; with blinding acceleration, to blast past other traffic on the few occasions when a clear, straight road presented itself; with powerful brakes, to reverse the effects of the aforementioned blinding acceleration; and at the end of it all, with a relatively modest cost because recovery from the Second World War was by no means complete, and overall prosperity was significantly lower than it is today. The only thing which was not particularly important was high-speed cruising ability, because there was hardly anywhere that you could cruise at high speed. Merely achieving "the ton" (100 mph/160 kph) was quite a feather in your cap; no-one expected to *cruise* at that kind of speed.

The bike which evolved to meet these specifications was the "café racer." The first, and easiest, modification was to remove absolutely everything that was not essential. Tool-boxes were simply jettisoned. Air-cleaners were replaced with short inlet stacks, with a wire mesh cover for vestigial protection: bore and carburetter wear from the dust was a problem, to say nothing of what might happen as a result of the occasionally ingested pebble. In the opposite direction, the chromed openwork mesh over the carburetter bellmouth acted as a frame-guard in the event of a backfire. Not only was there a significant weight saving in removing the air-cleaner: the engine also breathed easier, if not for as long.

A light-alloy tank saved a few pounds compared with the standard steel item, and if you were really into "added lightness" you might start drilling things like gear-levers, sprockets, etc., to save yet more weight: some café racers seemed to be adorned with steel and light-alloy lace, though more than one kick-start broke after being too enthusiastically lightened. Then again, a real café racer might have had the kick-start mechanism removed

LEFT: *Arlen Ness has a genius for building machines which look functional, even when a moment's thought tells you that the idea is about as practical as a barbed-wire bikini. This twin-belted blower Harley looks gorgeous, but "fast" and "Harley" are concepts which do not really fit together.*

FACING PAGE BOTTOM: *Slight "overs" promote straight-line stability and reduce tendencies to wheelie in drag races, but they also make low-speed handling very interesting indeed, and the longer they get, the worse they make the handling. They also mean you cannot use realistic front brakes, just tiny drums.*

altogether, saving more weight but forcing reliance on run-bump-and-vault starting.

The next trick was to go for the "racing crouch;" lower bars (preferably clip-ons that attached to the fork stanchions), and then rear-sets which moved the rider's feet backwards and (frequently) upwards. A barely-padded, plank-like seat with a hump or "bum-stop" at the back lowered the riding position and possibly even improved the aerodynamics. The reduction of frontal area, combined with the lightening of an already light bike, made for considerably more top-end urge.

After this, the engine might be "breathed upon." In the days when 30 bhp was powerful, 40 bhp off the shelf was *very* powerful, and 45-50 bhp was all you could hope for, there was a ready market for "go-faster" parts. At the very least, the inlet and exhaust tracts would be carefully cleaned up, to improve flow of fuel and air into the engine and to facilitate the escape of spent gases from it. A less restrictive (and rather noisier) exhaust pipe was *de rigeur*, even if nothing else was done to the engine to justify it. The carburetters would be re-jetted (as they would have to be, or the thing probably would not run any more) or even replaced, and the head might be skimmed to increase the compression ratio: in those days, you could still buy "five-star" petrol with a research octane of 101 – maybe 97 octane by the more honest American R+M/2 system.

If you were really serious, there were big-bore kits to increase the swept volume, albeit with the certainty of increased vibration together with the distinct possibility of overloading the bottom end and blowing up the engine. Or you might take a really powerful engine and put it into the ultimate frame, the wideline Featherbed. If you used a Triumph engine, you had a Triton; with a Vincent engine (which involved a small amount of sacrilegious carvery on the crank-cases), you had a Norvin. At least one enterprising gentleman, more interested in looks than in power, is alleged to have stuffed a Harley Panhead engine into a Featherbed, to make a Gnarley (the "G" was added for euphony).

The overall result was a motorcycle which was indeed very quick, very nimble, and very well-braked. It was also inclined to be deafeningly noisy and excruciatingly uncomfortable, which

ABOVE: *Is the Voyager a "custom" or a prototype? It traces its ancestry back to Malcolm Newell's Quasar and Royce Creasey's feet-forward specials, but it was always intended to be a production motorcycle.*

RIGHT: *The Blower Harley has all the hallmarks of Arlen Ness: stunning good looks, a (false) aura of practicality, and incredible technological overkill applied to the neolithic Harley V-twin motor. Amazingly enough, the beast is rideable and actually rather exciting, provided you do not encounter crosswinds, traffic, long distances or bends. It is not just the detailing which makes Arlen Ness bikes look so good: it is the remarkable thoroughness with which he devises and executes a concept, making it look like some weird museum piece from a lost civilization. And the thing is, he succeeds every time.*

LEFT: *It's a bird! It's a plane! It's a … no, it can't be … it's a V8 Cobra-powered tricycle! The logic, though, is unanswerable: if you are going to build a serious chop, why take the same tired old path that a hundred others have followed? A power-to-weight ratio that defies belief, rocket-like acceleration, no front brakes, and tiller steering – to say nothing of a turning circle like a Mack truck.*

ABOVE: *There is always a certain fascination in beautifully executed detail, and the detailing on this Harley is second to none. Even the exhaust pipe is engraved! But it still remains a very rideable motorcycle, though the small tank means you can't ride it very far. It even has twin front disks, which are normally the first thing to go on a custom bike.*

was why a number of people were a bit more restrained in their adoption of café racer features. The XLCR was such a motorcycle: at 520 lb it was really light for a Harley, but pretty heavy for anything else; and with its 61 cid (1000 cc) engine delivering a nominal 61 bhp, it could afford to be a bit heavier than a Triton. It was all black, it could run thirteen-second standing quarters, and it looked the business.

But that is, of course, only one direction that the customizer could take. Another direction is the "chopper."

These are the bikes that get custom cycles a bad name, even among fellow motorcyclists, and the classics were the stars of the movie *Easy Rider*: anyone who thought that Peter Fonda and Dennis Hopper had anything more than supporting roles clearly wasn't a motorcyclist.

The basic impulse was the same: the term "chopper" is said to come from the way that the excess was "chopped" off overweight (and sometimes stolen) Harley-Davidsons. A European might think that this was done in a desperate attempt to get a believable power-to-weight ratio, but in truth it seems that performance and handling were set aside in favour of sheer appearance. After all, "chopping" and "hot-rodding" motor-cars began during Prohibition, and well before "chopped" motorcycles came into fashion, those who favoured four-wheelers were busy drawing attention to themselves by doing outrageous things to automobiles. When form is more important than function, and appearance is more important than substance, it is only a matter of time before common sense goes out of the window.

Instead of the racing crouch, which is suitable for riding relatively short distances very quickly, American riders preferred what might be called the "laid back" position, which is suitable for riding relatively large distances very slowly. Instead of tucking the feet back, they are stretched forward; instead of lowering the handlebars and "tucking in," the rider fits "ape-hangers" or high-rise bars. And instead of the narrow, board-like solo seat with the bum-stop, the American rider coddles his rump with what looks like a tractor saddle, either carrying his "ol' lady" on an agonizingly small rectangular pad which would not look out of place on a 1921 Raleigh, or putting her on a species of pedestal: a plush, elevated platform, quite possibly with a back-rest.

At anything above fifty or sixty miles per hour (80-100 kph), the American riding position rapidly becomes literally untenable. The rider is spread-eagled in the wind, and hanging on becomes a chore. And this is *before* the customizers set to work and exaggerate all the problems, much as the builders of the café racers parodied the position of a racing rider.

The footrests, rechristened footpegs, are positioned so far forward and so high and wide that they immediately call to mind a gynaecologist's examining table, and the bars are raised so high that they have to recurve down again at the ends in order for the rider to be able to grip them: sudden acceleration can jerk his hands backwards and downwards off the bars.

Then, for completely inexplicable reasons, the front forks are lengthened, often dramatically. It is true that extended forks and increased trail make for greater straight-line stability, which is

desirable if you are planning continent-sized trips (though an astonishingly small percentage of American riders are much more than Sunday-afternoon motorcyclists, as witness the popularity of the "peanut" tank), but which makes turning distinctly tricky. Also, the enormously long forks which some riders installed were so weak that front brakes became impractical: anything much more powerful than a pedal-cycle brake would wind up the forks like a clock spring. A psychiatrist could probably make much of the fact that a chopper with extended forks and high-rise bars is reminiscent of nothing so much as a toddler's tricycle.

Finally, a vivid paint job completes the transformation. Many themes were lifted straight from custom cars, such as flames, fades, and deep, gleaming "kandy-kolor" metallic paints. Others were a poke in the eye for the bourgeoisie: American flags, skulls

ABOVE: *Is this the original Purple People Eater? Acres of bathroom acrylic, real arms for the armchair seat, tractor-style stack covers* (appropriately enough) *for the exhausts …. And people say Americans have no taste!*

and gravestones, and soft-core pornography or (at the very least) "pin-up" pictures.

Some of these custom paint jobs are absolutely stunning, and more and more motorcyclists are using the services of custom painters on more conventional motorcycles, whether for "murals" (the common term for paintings on tanks, or more rarely on fairings and side-panels) – and this brings yet another variety of custom cycle.

The "Detail Bike" *looks* like a very much more modest version of a full-blooded custom cycle; there is nothing that is outrageous, at least from a functional point of view, but there are things about the bike that are simply – well – *different*. When you change enough details, you may even end up with a "Special" – a bike which combines features (and parts!) from many manufacturers, blended with any luck into a harmonious whole.

At the very least there may be a new paint job, which may be anything from a subtle improvement on the original to full-blown "murals." Improving on the original paint job is not usually difficult; it is just very, very time consuming and (if you have someone do it for you) it can also be expensive. The trick lies in choosing the right colour – almost any colour is better than some of the late 1960s colours from, say, Triumph – and then in putting on many, many coats, each individually hand-rubbed before the next is applied. On top of that, clear-coat enamel gives still more depth: a properly-done custom paint job gives the impression that you are looking into a deep jewel. It is an odd sensation, and not one that is easily explained.

Parts can be plated and polished, too – though you have to be careful about this, as some of the more traditionally-minded motorcycle manufacturers in Europe take advantage of the heat-dissipating qualities of sand-cast light alloy, and polishing or plating can lead to distinct cooling problems. Also, not all finishes are suitable for all parts of a motorcycle. Frames, for example, can be nickelled but should not be chromed, because chroming will embrittle the frame tubing. And gold-plating is almost invariably ugly and "over the top." You can, however, replace a lot of parts with stainless steel, to the benefit of both looks and durability, and sometimes performance as well; braided stainless steel brake lines not only look good but can actually improve braking efficiency.

FACING PAGE TOP: *This Triumph X65 Special is one of those styling exercises you either love or hate. Those who love it point to the style-setting tank/seat unit and argue that it has dramatically changed the appearance of a motorcycle that everyone knows and loves. Those who hate it say exactly the same thing. It has been said that Triumphs are England's Harleys, which is true to some extent; but it is also true that the Triumph is a small, light, slim, well-designed motorcycle which is simply less amenable than the Harley to being hacked about or hung with gew-gaws. Subtlety is the key to most Triumph customs.*

RIGHT: *If Harleys handled as badly as most people say, there would not be so many greybeards riding them; or maybe it's the other way around, and riding Harleys turns the beards of even 25-year-olds grey.*

It is, however, interesting that while (for example) BMW or Laverda riders are mostly content with the handling, engines and appointments that the manufacturers give them, Harley-Davidson owners do not seem to be happy until they have modified their machines away from what the gentlemen in Milwaukee intended. Sometimes, it seems, it is all but impossible to find two Harleys that are alike.

RIGHT: *Some people would argue that customizing old, rigid-framed motorcycles such as this Indian is heresy; as "classics," such bikes should be left in original condition. But remember: today's classic is yesterday's old bike, and what is wrong with customizing old bikes? The only answer, surely, must come down to good taste; and while the front end of this Indian is not in keeping with the rest of the bike and adds nothing in the way of modern handling (as usual, there is no front brake), its owner presumably likes it, and he is keeping it on the road. Also, anyone who can ride a bike with a foot clutch, especially with a young lady balanced precariously on the rear mudguard, must be some kind of hero.*

Then there are things on any bike which are not quite right: ugly silencers (mufflers), perhaps, such as the "ray-guns" on the early Triumph Trident triples, which looked like something out of a peculiarly low-budget 1950s science fiction movie. You could change these in a dozen ways: "meggas" for a café racer look, "Brooklands cans," or the old-fashioned, pipe-bulge-pipe style for a vintage look, ultra-modern "coffee-can" styles, or even pipes painted with heat-resisting "header" paint in fire-engine red. Although stainless silencers are a great idea, stainless down-pipes (headers) are arguably another matter; they will soon discolour to a rather sickly yellow, which many people find very unattractive. Chrome won't last as long, and it will discolour too, but at least it discolours to prettier colours. I don't know if it would be possible to make titanium down-pipes, but it's an interesting idea. That stuff discolours all the colours of the rainbow!

Or maybe it's not the silencers you don't like. Maybe it's the oil-tank, which you could replace with a stainless-steel item perhaps. Or maybe it's the saddle: you can buy a saddle ready-made from someone like Mike Corbin, or you can have your own old seat-pan re-covered. You could choose anything from a racing "bum-stop" to a Harley-esque "King and Queen," with enormous rump-coddling apprentice armchairs. And, of course, it doesn't have to be dull black.

Another area where changes are easy is mudguards. Do you want a skimpy, classical alloy or chrome front mudguard? Or something deeply valanced and vintage looking? How about "bobbing" or shortening the rear mudguard – or, for a really practical vintage touch, installing a hinged rear mudguard for easy wheel-changing. Incidentally, although some American terms make more sense than the English, such as "muffler" instead of "silencer" (which one is more accurate, after all?), anyone who thinks that a mudguard is a fender shouldn't be allowed on a

motorcycle. Can you imagine *trying* to "fend off" anything with a motorcycle mudguard? You'd be in the gutter in a trice.

What else? 'Bars, of course, whether you prefer more rise, or flatter bars or even clip-ons. Switchgear, for looks, ergonomics, and reliability. Mirrors: 'bar-end mirrors may be vulnerable if you fall off, but they provide excellent visibility. Wheels: alloy wheels run truer, and are stronger – but if they do break, you have to replace the whole thing, while you can lace virtually anything onto a sound hub with a spoked wheel. And many people prefer the looks of wires, even if they are heavier and harder to clean. Fairings are a matter of taste, but you can fit anything from a full-size "dolphin" fairing (or even a 1950s-style racing "dustbin" fairing, for that matter) to a handlebar-mounted windshield to the little "bikini" fairing that was popularized by BMW with the R90S. And if your bike already has a fairing, how about a new windshield? Higher, lower, smoked, or even neon-coloured; think of Zero Gravity and their vividly-coloured offerings.

This kind of thing can be continued indefinitely. Some "details" involve fairly major surgery, such as changing the front forks; this used to be a particularly popular trick when most of the subjects for detailing were British bikes of the 1960s, afflicted with drum brakes. Discs might not look so traditional, but they certainly made the bike stop better. Today, "White Power" or similar shock absorbers can improve both the handling and the looks of the rear end. Sooner or later, you edge over into the "special," and you may even decide to replace the manufacturer's original frame with (say) a Harris or Bimota frame in order to get the kind of handling that is needed to tame the more insanely-powerful engines.

There can be new details under the skin, as well. Taking the staid BMW as an example, the flywheel could be lightened. The penalty will be rougher power delivery at low speeds, and possibly a higher tickover as well; but the benefit will be significantly quicker throttle response. The heads can be gas-flowed: there is a limit to what is commercially feasible during production, but skilled after-work can make the engine breathe more freely. Stronger valve springs and titanium push-rods mean that the motor will rev. faster, and keep pulling at higher revs: done properly, the conservative old 7250 rpm bloodline can be increased to as much as 8000 rpm. Increased compression ratios are possible if you twin-plug the head, or you could buy a pair of Krauser 4-valve heads "off the shelf." And even BMW themselves forsook their beloved Bing CV carbs on the R90S, for Dell 'Ortos with slide throttles. Some people will "hot up" a respectable-looking bike and deliberately keep all the styling cues even more respectable; quite apart from the pleasures of riding a motorcycle that is more powerful than anyone has a right to expect from its looks, there is less chance of being pulled over. If you look respectable, it's amazing what you can get away with ….

Generally, though, subtlety is where it's at. When it is finished, a "detail" bike or "special" should not look outlandish: it should simply look like the best bike of that particular make and model that you ever saw. Everything about it will be right, and it is only as you begin to look more closely that you realize how far the owner may have diverged from the manufacturer's original. That almost standard-looking BMW R100RS; what has been done to it? Ah, yes; the owner has fitted rear-sets, to lift his feet up and backwards into a more racy riding position, and the whole character of the motorcycle is subtly changed.

Other people are not into subtlety. The café racer, the chopper, the ultra-vivid "art school" paint job are their thing. And there is a whole school of motorcycle customizing which apparently believes that nothing succeeds like excess. These are the "full dresser" crowd.

"Full Dressers" are primarily American, and the technique is simple. You start with a monster motorcycle – and then you add

BELOW: *Daytona during Bike Week is the place to see really unusual motorcycles – and, of course, tricycles. The majority of trikes are based on Volkswagen engines, and standard frames and even bodywork are available "off the shelf." The only scope for true customizing at this point is the paint – which anyone would have to admit has been rather handsomely executed here – and the detailing, which on this bike could use a little more attention: the windshield/ weather shield treatment on the front forks is somewhat at variance with the rest of the machine. In most of Europe, more attention is also paid to such mundane matters as making the motorcycle stop: front brakes are a (not unreasonable) legal requirement.*

on more. Not content with the stereo cassette deck, the AM/FM radio, and the Citizens' Band radio, you add a cellular telephone *and answering machine* (it was already available at the time of writing). The radar detector is taken for granted, as is the cruise control. But how about adjustable foot-warmers? The idea is that in cold weather you divert some of the engine heat that would otherwise be wasted in the general direction of your tootsies. The motorcycle's onboard air compressor takes care of setting the air-assisted suspension.

The hard-shell luggage is probably supplied with the bike, but in order to protect it you might decide to add crash bars around the outside. While you're at it, you can put other assorted crash-bars, rubbing strakes and telaros on either side. Of course, you can't risk the seats getting wet, so you always carry a seat cover (some bikes provide them as standard equipment).

At least the majority of this stuff bears some faint relationship to functionality, and so (for that matter) may a couple of extra lights, but the excess of running lights, so that the machine lights up like a Christmas tree, is another matter entirely. Some people use the little, old "bullet" style lights that are still available in accessory shops, the sort that used to be used for tail-lights and indicator-lights on motor-cars, while others buy light strips from custom suppliers; you can even buy number plate surrounds where the lights follow one another in a "ripple" pattern, like something from a Las Vegas casino. Most people who go to this degree of excess are not too bright, so they don't check the charging capacity of their motorcycle; they therefore tend to have a lot of trouble with flat batteries and burned-out alternators. The old rule that "Watts = Volts x Amps" is alien to them. Some people are as addicted to rear-view mirrors as others are to a plethora of lights; presumably, when their bikes tip over they can contemplate with equanimity the prospect of anything from twenty-eight to seventy-seven years of bad luck.

And make no mistake, these monsters tip over. On many U.S. tours, the baggage-and-breakdown wagon that follows the motorcyclists is very unlikely to have any trouble with these enormously reliable, utterly understressed motorcycles, but apparently they can rely on broken ankles incurred when the riders try to stop their behemoths toppling. The stock weight of a 1992 Honda Gold Wing GL1500/6 Special Edition was 890 lb. (404.5 Kg) with all fluids, and it was not difficult to add another 40-50 lb. (say 20 Kg) in accessories.

Now add a modest amount of luggage – another 40-50 lb. or 20 Kg – and something very interesting happens. The maximum permitted gross vehicle weight of that same Honda is 1283 lb. (583 Kg), and *before you put the rider on* you already have an all-up weight of 980 lb. or 445 Kg. While even the fattest Goldwing rider, fully clad, is unlikely much to exceed 303 lb/138 Kg, the most cursory glance at some of the couples who ride "full dressers" shows that they are profoundly unlikely to weigh as little as 150 lb each; 200-250 lb (say 100 Kg) each, fully suited and

ABOVE: *the true Harley rider is as carefully turned out as his mount: the helmet is as much a matter of style as of protection, aviator glasses and bandannas are all but compulsory, and slogans like LIVE TO RIDE are as much a part of the lifestyle as H-D teeshirts, leathers, wallets, mugs, keyrings ….*

RIGHT: *The palace of the Maharaja of Mysore is said to be lit with three lakhs (300,000) of light bulbs; perhaps the rider of this AMF-era Harley always wanted to be a Maharaja. Half the power of the engine must be expended on keeping the lights burning, and half the rider's time must be spent replacing bulbs.*

helmeted, would be nearer the mark. This means that even such a monster as the big 'Wing is commonly ridden overloaded, and that its mass on the move can easily exceed 1400 lb, 636 Kg. And that's before you add (as many "Full Dress" riders do) a trailer ....

Before we leave customs, there are two other phenomena which deserve brief mention: scooters, and rat bikes.

Scooters like the Vespa and Lambretta are known to many traditionalist motorcyclists as "hair dryers," but there is no doubt that they can be (and have been) heavily customized. Chromed side panels, a bevy of mirrors and running lights (which their puny generators are even worse equipped to supply than is a motorcycle's), Union Jack paint jobs, fur-covered seats, a multiplicity of aerials adorned with flags and fake squirrel-tails; you can do almost anything with a scooter except make it handle ....

As for "rat bikes," these are rarely planned: they just happen. A rat bike is the cheapest, nastiest ride-to-work bike imaginable, and it receives the bare minimum of maintenance that is necessary to keep in on the road. No gleaming silencers here: solid rust, more likely, with the holes patched with bean-cans and baling wire (or beer cans and Jubilee clips, for the more stylish). Paint is retouched (if at all) with primer, with odds and ends of whatever you have in the cupboard, and with Hammerite. Gobs of foam hang out of the slashed seat; outlying appurtenances such as indicators and the balls on the end of the control levers are simply abandoned when they fail, fall off, or are knocked off. In theory, the "rat bike" is what you ride while you are lovingly restoring your Speed Twin, or WLC, or Comet. In practice, it's an art form in its own right.

BELOW: *Double-engined Harley dragsters are one thing; double-engined Harley road bikes are quite another, No wonder the rider is a big man!*

BELOW: *Harley-Davidson's original three-wheeler, the Servi-Car, was intended as a breakdown truck! Since then, there have been many trikes, though few have been as functional as the original.*

CUSTOM

RIGHT: *V8-engined bikes and trikes are an enduring fascination, but this one is particularly interesting because of the remote steering. This allows considerably quicker, easier control of the front forks, but it must still be more than a little demanding to ride. Everything about this improbable bike is beautifully done: look at the clutch bell-housing, for example.*

BELOW: *It's a Nortwart – or you could call it a Wartnort, a Warton or a Norberg. Over the years, enterprising specials builders have stuffed just about everything into a Norton frame, but this 3-cylinder Wartburg engine must be one of the most original machines of all time. The East German two-stroke motor may not be too impressive in a car, but it is quite potent in motorcycle terms.*

ABOVE: *this would surely be the perfect bike for a pianist in a whorehouse. It has the perfect New Orleans over-the-top attention to detail: opulence at any cost. The real joke is that in the original picture, a man admiring the bike is wearing a T-shirt* which says, RATHER A SISTER IN THE WHOREHOUSE THAN A BROTHER ON A HONDA.

BELOW: *The (so-called) Indian Brave is actually a British-* built two-stroke, but if the owner leaves it out in the rain for long enough, preferably at the sea-side, the light alloy can grow white scabs and the rust can get a bit more of a hold, turning it into a real rat. Right now, it's a bit too pretty to qualify.

CUSTOM

BELOW: "Murals" – paintings on gas tanks, side panels, mudguards and more – are usually executed with an airbrush, and vary widely in quality. Hard-masked paintings are rare: this is either soft-masked or freehand. This is a very common theme, the Barbarian Prince and Princess, but it is clear that the artist (from John's Custom Paint in New Hampshire) had been requested to get a bit too much in: a simpler design, with fewer elements, would have enabled him/her to work on a larger, more dramatic scale and to execute the details more carefully. Paintings like this rarely look as good in photographs as they do in real life; a photograph cannot seem to record the sheer illusion of depth in the paint.

LEFT: *Black leather is undoubtedly a practical, abrasion-resistant material for riding clothes; and studs add still more abrasion resistance when used in the right places. The relevance of chains to motorcycles is clear, too. But quite apart from all that, the "biker look" clearly has an appeal all of its own.*

LEFT: *Black leather is undoubtedly a practical, abrasion-resistant material for riding clothes; and studs add still more abrasion resistance when used in the right places. The relevance of chains to motorcycles is clear, too. But quite apart from all that, the "biker look" clearly has an appeal all of its own.*

ABOVE: *The longer you look at this bike, the more you realize how very little remains of the original Harley-Davidson from which it evolved. Like all the most successful chops, the bike "works" because of the consistency of the theme: a sort of Christmassy richness, like Russian miniature enamel-work. The detailing is exquisite: look at the rear mudguard stay, for example, or the pinstriping on the rear forks. Gold has been used wherever it is needed, and yet still with restraint: the contrast between chrome and gold is extremely well balanced, where a less confident builder might have over-used it or (at the very least) used it in the wrong places. The front forks are not so over-extended that the bike cannot be ridden, but with a front end like that, headstock angles are critical.*

RIGHT: *Mother-of-pearl and "flip-flop" effects (which change colour when viewed from different angles) are among the most expensive and difficult to achieve; some paints actually use fish-scales to give the desired effect. Because these paints are so difficult to use, it is usually only the very best custom painters who even try, and the effects they achieve are often very good indeed. In the photograph, this effect is impressive: in the original, it is nothing short of stunning. The extensive engraving on the engine is impressive, too, but the richness of the effect is somewhat let down by the clear plastic fuel pipe. The next stage, surely, would be stainless steel (or even gold plated) braided hose for the fuel lines.*

LEFT: *Stop thinking in terms of applied art: this is surely fine art. Whether you can ride it or not – and you probably can – the magnificent double-engined Harley special is a masterpiece of ingenuity. It is also very noticeable that the paint job is brilliantly conceived to frame the engines, which are after all the main point of the exercise, rather than distracting attention from them. To cap it all, there are some interesting practical details such as the remote, apparently hub-centre steering. It is not clear whether there is a fuel pump to lift fuel from the forward gas tank, or whether the alarmingly vulnerable-looking carburettors are gravity fed in the usual fashion.*

CUSTOM

RIGHT: *Yes, but what happens in the event of a crash stop? One of the reasons that Triumph eventually dropped those nifty little luggage racks on the tank was apparently the risk of riders castrating themselves in an accident. Many custom bikes draw on the same inspiration as "heavy metal" music (which is logical, when you consider what a Harley weighs), and the theme of death/skulls/ demons/graveyards is often encountered, though rarely executed so skilfully as here. The detailing is impressive: look at the "tendrils" behind the tank.*

ABOVE: *The Stars and Stripes are a classic theme for decorating Harleys, and here they are used to very good effect, together with another traditional icon, the All-American Girl – even if she is not wearing clothing suitable for motorcycling. The overall effect is a classic, though not exactly on the cutting edge of new design. Motorcyclists have rarely been known for their political correctness, which is how frankly sexist pictures like this manage to survive; but sexist or not, it is beautifully executed, and who could really take exception?*

ABOVE: "Flame" designs are one of the oldest and most popular themes in custom painting – and one of the most difficult to execute. Here, the painter has used every trick in the book to very good effect: the colours are beautifully matched, the gradations of colour inside the main flames are very well done, and the overpainting adds the final touch.

RIGHT: Figuring out the meaning of personalized license plates can while away many a tedious car journey. Is Hank dyslexic? Is there some sort of pun, HAM from a Hog? What would you choose? We had KHYUNG in California (Tibetan for the Celestial Hawk – it was a Guzzi), but they would not let me have RED PIG. They said it was not respectful to the police!

ABOVE: *Few non-professional customizers work in this degree of luxury: plenty of room, plenty of light, and a tool chest that many full-time mechanics would envy. The caption to this picture by well-known bike photographer Mike Lichter reads, "Building bikes in my garage." Note the difference between the "hardtail" (rigid) frame on the table and the one on the floor.*

LEFT: *One of the less expected aspects of the American biking scene is girls in "thong" bikinis. Despite the poor abrasion resistance of such outfits, they wear them on motorcycles. Fun-loving Sonny Bono, formerly of Sonny and Cher and now mayor of Palm Springs, has tried to ban both motorcycles and thongs during Easter Week, when the town traditionally fills up with students.*

BELOW: *This olive-drab, pseudo-military rat trike is superbly executed. It looks as if it might once have been a Servi-Car, but if it was, it has been extensively modified with twin discs, a different engine, replacement bars and a lot more. In many countries, trikes give rise to an interesting legal dilemma: if they are cars, you have to wear seat belts, and if they are bikes, you have to wear a helmet. But what if they are both? Or neither? Carrying as many as four people is no problem: in Delhi, there are Servi-Cars that have been converted to taxis, the 45 cid Harley engines long ago replaced with single-cylinder hand-start diesels. The frames seem virtually indestructible: eight or ten passengers are quite usual.*

5
RACING & SPORT

Racing motorcycles is dangerous, irresponsible, expensive, and of increasingly limited relevance to roadgoing motorcycling. It is also fun.

On this fundamental contradiction is built an enormous variety of two-wheeled competition. There is of course GP racing; perhaps the definitive form of the sport, but for most of us a spectator activity rather than one in which we can participate. Then there is what used to be called "clubman's" racing; the sort of (almost) affordable racing that the AJS 7R and the Goldie were built for. Or there is vintage racing, where AJS 7R "Boys' Racers" and Goldies and Manx Nortons and Comets and KTT Velocettes and all the other magical names of the past compete, all in their respective classes. Or there is Twin racing, where (for the most part) V-twins wipe the floor with BMW Boxers and souped-up parallel twins. Then there is sidecar racing, where demented gentlemen (few ladies are crazy enough for this sport) do very fair impersonations of a monkey on a stick while pretending to be passengers in exiguous outfits which are so low that the rider is effectively kneeling four inches off the deck. There is flat-track racing, also known as speedway racing, where the oval monotony of the circuit is compensated for by the incredible angles of lean achieved by the foot-dragging riders, and then there is ice racing, where ferociously-spiked tyres allow even more unbelievable riding styles. And there used to be board-track or short-track racing, which was even more confined and even more dangerous. The various forms of dirt racing have already been touched upon, apart from the curious modern form of hill-climbing where extra-long rear swinging arms and "paddle" tyres have replaced the dirt bikes of old; and then there are drag bikes. And this is without

Ian Simpson leads Jim Moore out of the corner (left) while Kevin Schwanz (above) also demonstrates the technique of riding with the knees as far apart as possible – and although a discreet "S" tells you that Kevin is on a Suzuki, you really have to be an insider to know what anyone else is riding.

even considering speed-record attempts as a form of racing, which it surely is, though against the clock rather than against the competitor alongside.

From a roadgoing perspective, there is one race which stands so far above all the others that it must be considered alone: the Isle of Man Tourist Trophy. The original 1905 International Cup was run over a 16-mile circuit which was shortened from the 37.75 mile Gordon Bennett race, but the first real Tourist Trophy was held in 1907. The "Tourist" part of the title came from the fact that it was an event for what might today be called "street" (or possibly "silhouette") motorcycles, which were theoretically equipped for touring: they were expected to be equipped with such niceties as saddles, mudguards, brakes on both wheels and tool boxes, and the singles had to be able to cover at least 90 mpg (the Imperial or full gallon, of course; this is a mere 72 miles to the short, or American, gallon.) Twins and other multis were allowed to guzzle fuel at 75 mpg. Rather than a mass start, riders were released in pairs every minute (an interval later shortened to a mere ten seconds), so timing was as important as who actually crossed the line first. The reason that the Island was originally chosen was that the House of Keys, the Manx parliament, was willing to close public roads for road racing – something at which the Mother of Parliaments at Westminster always jibbed.

The history of the Island is glorious, and for the next sixty years or so it was to be the premier showcase for road/racing motorcycles. Charlie Collier won the first T.T. on his own Matchless 500, with a J.A.P. engine, while Rembrandt Fowler took the multi-cylinder title on a Norton with a Peugeot engine. The twin was a couple of miles an hour slower than the Matchless, which averaged no less than 38.5 mph and 94.5 mpg over the 10-lap, 160-mile course; a gruelling four and a quarter hours in the saddle. In 1911 the much longer "full" or "mountain" course of the old Gordon Bennett race, and the new inclines and hairpins, accelerated the development of multi-speed transmissions: that was the year in which the Americans scooped the pool with a 1-2-3 win for

ABOVE: *Mike Van Vries rides a 1962 Manx Norton: no sponsors' stickers, no art-school graphics, and a discreetly lettered "piss-pot" helmet. No wonder old fogeys praise vintage racing; it's a lot closer to "real-world" riding.*

BELOW: *The basic premise of sidecar racing was always a bit strange, rather like truck racing or lawnmower racing; but it is still a thrilling spectacle. This Manx Norton outfit was formerly raced by Charlie Freeman.*

ABOVE: *Hans Haldeman puts a "cammy" Norton through its paces. Details abound: what appears to be a disc brake on the back is a "bacon slicer" cooling fin, while the front brakes are twin-leading-shoe. For all its racing heritage, the "double knocker" is still very close to street-legal.*

RIGHT: *Velocette's supercharged "Roarer" might have pointed the way ahead for racing motorcycles if the Second World War had not intervened; as it was the "turbo" craze held off for about another four decades. An unusual feature, seldom remarked, is the shaft final drive.*

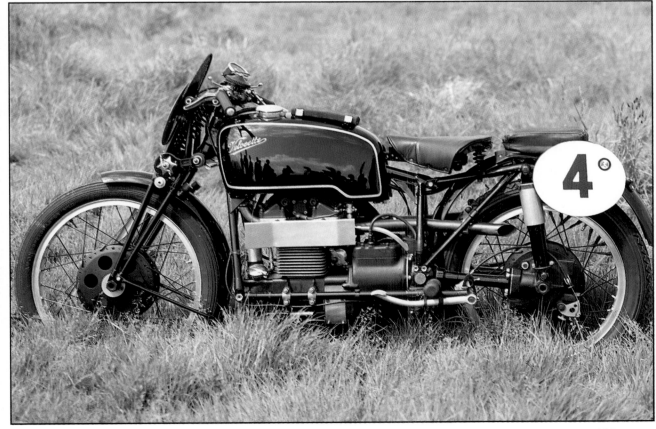

Indians equipped with 585cc V-twins, "free engine" (clutch) and two-speed countershaft gearboxes. In 1914 Peugeot raced twin-cam, four-valve parallel twins (the sort of thing the Japanese would boast about more than half a century later), while after the War to End Wars overhead-cam singles appeared from J.A.P. (1922), Velocette (1924), Norton (1928) and Sunbeam (1929). The Ricardo four-valve head, albeit with push-rod operated valves, appeared as early as 1921. Velocette introduced the positive-stop, foot-change gear shift in 1925, and hand changes were immediately rendered obsolete for both racing and road riding – though Harley-Davidson continued to regard hand-change as standard well after World War Two, and hand changes could be ordered from Milwaukee as a regular option for at least three decades after Velocette had shown the way forwards. In 1922, the winning speed of the T.T. was slightly under 52 mph (about 83 kph); by 1930, it had been raised to more than 74 mph (about 120 kph).

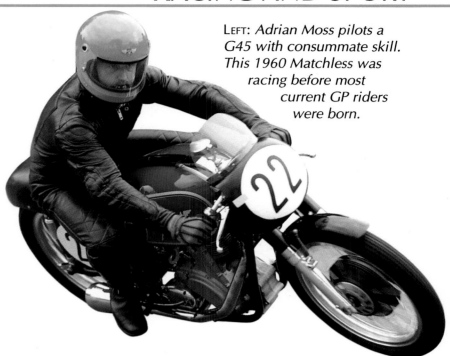

LEFT: *Adrian Moss pilots a G45 with consummate skill. This 1960 Matchless was racing before most current GP riders were born.*

There was then a period during which the hypertrophied single – "hypertrophied" in both the developmental sense and the sense of how many trophies it won – kept the edge over the multis, despite the theoretical advantages of the latter, partly from reliability, partly from the excellence of their frames (especially the Norton "Featherbed"), and partly by the skill of their riders; but even in the 1930s the twins were in with more than a chance (a blown BMW twin won the Senior in 1939), and by the 1950s the day of the 500cc single slowly passed. By the 1960s there was no longer any real contest. The MV Agusta 500cc ohc in-line four could deliver 70 bhp at 10,500 rpm: Honda's 500cc four had 15 bhp more at 11,000 rpm, but the Italian frame kept the MV Agusta competitive. The Norton, on the other hand, was strained beyond the limits of credibility to extract 52 bhp from a single cylinder at 7,000 rpm. When you compare 104 bhp with 140 bhp, it is clear that the singles' day was gone.

A curious thing happened, though. The lap record at the Island was raised to 99.97 mph in 1955 – as near to 100 mph (160 kph) as made no difference – but it started to become clear that as the twins and (particularly) MV Agusta's fours became faster and faster and more and more specialized, they began to lose their relevance to the everyday rider. In the first place, the bikes were becoming too alien to the everyday rider (who still regarded a single as normal, and a parallel twin as hot stuff). In the second place, they were simply becoming too fast. To ride a motorcycle

at 100 mph on a reasonably clear road is not that difficult; at 120 mph you are surprised at how fast the curves come up; and at 140 mph you are astonished to learn that roads you always regarded as straight are really quite twisty. In order to lap the Island at 100 mph you have to take everything at speeds which are literally inconceivable to the road rider.

Not only were they becoming too fast for the road rider: "Senior" bikes were becoming too fast for the professionals, too. On a modern race-track conditions are as forgiving as they can be to anyone who falls off at very high speeds, and if you know how to fall you can escape with remarkably light injuries even if you meet with misfortune at speeds significantly more than a mile a minute (100 kph). On the Island, though, there are no run-off areas and trackside perimeters, and straw bales are at best padding rather than the only obstruction you might meet. There were (and are) walls and trees and earth banks, as well as public houses and other exceptionally unyielding and unforgiving things to hit. Also, in place of a carefully-maintained track, there was (and is) just regular everyday road, with its share of hump-backed bridges and road markings and manhole covers and just plain old ripples and crud.

LEFT: *TEAM OBSOLETE, the tank proclaims. On the other hand, the skills required to race machines like this 500cc G50 Matchless are far from obsolete, and addicts of vintage racing love the sight and the sound of skilled riders on "real" motorcycles that you can see through.*

RIGHT: *This 1955 works Norton, with a "laid-down" engine, shows that while Norton were prepared to experiment, they saw the future very differently from their Italian (and later, Japanese) rivals. You can also see where some of the styling cues for the Rotary came from.*

RACING AND SPORT

The result, in the long run, was that the T.T. was dropped from the Grand Prix calendar, and became an entirely separate race on its own; though it has to be said that to this day, to many true motorcyclists, a so-called racer who does not compete at the Island is seen as lacking in a number of departments. This is so, even though those fans who cry loudest for the T.T. are often those who could barely complete the course on a moped without falling off and hurting themselves. But we do not all hold our heroes to (very much) higher standards than we hold ourselves: on "Mad Sunday," before the Senior, there are plenty of motorcyclists who see what they can do on the fabled Mountain Circuit. As often as not, one or two die finding out.

Since the glory days of the T.T (and a few other "round-the-houses" races on the Continent), motorcycle racing has declined to being a very much less popular spectator sport than Formula One car racing, though at the time of writing there were signs that this might be about to change; the FIM (*Fédération International Motocycliste*, since 1904 the ruling body of the sport) was being edged out by Bernie Ecclestone's Two Wheel Promotions (TWP) and the Spanish *Dorna Promócion del Deporte*, both of whom were promising very much bigger prize money, supported by the International Road Racing Teams Association (IRTA). With international television promotion, and *much* bigger purses, it is extremely likely that there will be a major revival.

Despite this, all kinds of extraordinary technological innovations have been tried by the Japanese, partly as publicity, partly because racing really does improve the breed, and partly from a uniquely Japanese attitude about "face." Soichiro Honda was a four-stroke man, and Honda's corporate policy was therefore always to race four-strokes, even though the volumetric efficiency of a two-stroke is inherently greater (you get a power stroke on every revolution from every cylinder). This led to some technological wonders such as the 1964 250/6, with its six tiny 42cc cylinders, and the 1965 125/5, with five 25cc cylinders. Later, there was the all but unbelievable "NR" series of V-fours with pistons which are so oval as to have been called oblong, but which allow a mind-boggling eight valves per cylinder and a power band which runs between about 10,000 and 20,000 rpm. And still the two-strokes continued to win ….

With reliable street bikes delivering well over 100 bhp/litre in the early 1970s – Yamaha's 195cc two-stroke twin of 1972 delivered 22 bhp at 7,500 rpm, almost 113 bhp/litre – it is clear that the more highly-strung and fragile machines for "clubman" racing were also getting very, very quick indeed. Increasing affluence also meant that more and more racers could afford more and more specialized machines, which in turn meant that fewer and fewer "ordinary" motorcyclists followed club racing. It had always been cliquey; now, the clique was tiny. In April 1992, for example, *Cycle World* was able to sing the praises of the Rotax-engined Aprilia AF-1 250cc two-stroke V-twin, calling it an incredible bargain at "around $38,000." This for a 200-lb. motorcycle with carbon-fibre bodywork and handlebars, a titanium filler cap, and more than 80 bhp; about twice the power of a Goldie with 150 lb. less weight. Yes, its performance is staggering, but for that price you could buy a new BMW K100RS *and* a Harley FLTC *and* a Honda VFR750RS and still have some change left over. This is not mainstream motorcycling.

RIGHT: *The Isle of Man Senior Tourist Trophy is simply the ultimate road race: real racing on real roads, with real motorcycles. Yes, it is dangerous, but to die-hard fans of the Island, anyone who refuses to ride the* Mountain Circuit on the grounds of safety alone is not fit to ride anywhere, let alone to call himself a racer. Here, Goodley and Hunt are neck and neck at Creg-na-Baa in the 1992 Senior.

LEFT: *Sidecar racing requires a special brand of hero at the best of times: modern "kneeler" outfits suspend the rider very close to the tarmac, and the "monkey on a stick" antics of the passenger are truly hair-raising. But racing outfits at the Island (this is the Roy Hanks/Tom Hanks outfit at the 1991 Sidecar TT) requires even more courage: a misjudged corner can result in violent and possibly terminal contact with stone walls and other unforgiving surfaces. Even experienced motorcyclists sometimes watch the races like a child watching cartoons: covering their eyes with their hands when disaster seems inevitable, then peeking between their fingers to see what happened.*

It is because of this sort of thing that restricted classes, such as (more or less) stock twins, and vintage racing, have become popular.

In a sense, a twin is a retrograde step when straight-four and V-four engines are commonplace in road bikes, but even so there are significant advantages for both riders and spectators. For the rider, even a fully hopped up BMW or Ducati or whatever is a lot cheaper and easier to work on than a from-the-ground-up racing bike. They are also slower, which (to some extent) means that they are safer. For the spectators, "real" bikes look better, sound better, and can be more closely identified with their own machines than a titanium-and-carbon-fibre oval-piston monster costing $60,000 or more.

The same is true of vintage racing, though there is an enormous difference between racing vintage machines now, and racing them when they were new, and that difference is tyres. Modern rubber is so much stickier that many vintage racers are actually faster now (in lap times, not absolute top speed) than they were when they were new. They can be laid over further in the corners, and braked harder and later, without anything like as high a risk of losing traction as would have been the case when they were first built. Even so, it is hard to suppress a shudder when you think of the value of (say) a Vincent Black Lightning, and see the apparent abandon with which a vintage racer may pilot it.

But road-racing, whether real round-the-houses road racing or track racing, and whether with state-of-the-art bikes or twins or vintage machines, is not everything. It probably attracts more interest in Europe, where high-speed riding on sweet-handing motorcycles can (if you have the time) be an everyday experience. In the United States, where the vast majority of roads are flat and wide and boring and where incredibly low speed limits are savagely (if capriciously) enforced, the focus of the everyday motorcyclist is not on top speed or handling; it is in simple, straight-line brute acceleration. The "standing quarter" and the terminal speed are the be-all and end-all of most American motorcyclists' horizons, and indeed top speeds are frequently ignored in road tests. In Europe, the 0-60 mph or 0-100 kph time is the measure of acceleration, and one might think that this was more relevant to real-world riding than covering a quarter of a mile from a standing start. This is especially true in light of the fact that terminal velocities for modern 750cc motorcycles are mostly in the 100 to 120 mph range – 160 to 190 kph – a good way to get thrown in jail if you are caught doing this on an American public road. But for some extraordinary reason, possibly the profusion of stop signs which occur every few blocks (and sometimes every block) in the United States, brute acceleration is everything.

This is why a large number of downright terrifying motorcycles have been so successful in the American market: the old Kawasaki two-stroke "flexi-flyer" 500cc and 750cc triples spring to mind, though the Yamaha V-Max with its awesome 145 bhp is arguably in the same category. The theoretical top speeds of these machines are just that: theoretical, because no-one could hold on to the wildly unergonomic 'bars for more than a few seconds at top speed, and besides, the top speed could only be explored on a very straight, very flat, very wide road. Even the V-Max, though orders of magnitude better than the 1960s Kwackers, is not a motorcycle to be ridden fast: it is a motorcycle to be *accelerated* fast.

And inevitably, just as road-racing bikes have become increasingly specialized, so have dragsters. While a typical 750cc machine can pull standing quarters in the eleven-, twelve- and thirteen-second range, and while some 1000cc motorcycles can break the 10-second barrier, purpose-built dragsters have broken the 7-second barrier. It is worth knowing, incidentally, that "six second quarters" does not mean (as the non-*aficionado* might think) "six seconds or less" but "six-point-something seconds." Thus even a 6.95 second quarter is a "six second quarter."

Dragsters are mostly very long, to counteract the natural tendency to pull "wheelies" when anything up to 1000 bhp is suddenly unleashed on the asphalt, and "wheelie bars" also resist flipping. Fuels are rarely anything so prosaic as gasoline: at the very least, very high octane gasoline will be enlivened with

ABOVE: *If you can't compete at the Island, at least you can ride around the circuit; and that is precisely what happens on Mad Sunday, when visitors to the TT test their skills against the Mountain Circuit. Perhaps* astonishingly, *fatalities are few – but they can and do happen. A true fanatic would not care: he would already be in Paradise when he died.*

ABOVE: *The television audience will see more of the race than the fans who wait out along the course, but they will not hear the true music of the machines, growing from a low thrumming in the distance to an ear-shattering roar as another rider flashes past, nor will they smell the summer air laden with oil and exhaust fumes. It is the difference between hearing a recording of a piece of music, and being present at the concert. This is the 1991 TT.*

RIGHT: *Laps at 100 mph (160 kph) have been possible on the Island for decades – but there is a great difference between a dry road on a sunny day, and a road where the machine in front throws up just enough mist and mud to obscure your visor, but not enough to bead and roll off. The rider is constantly at the limits of adhesion, and the passenger has to have even more faith than usual in the pilot's skills.*

BELOW AND RIGHT: *Joey Dunlop's fourteenth TT win, in 1991, brought him level with Mike Hailwood's record. Although the Senior is the best-known and most hotly contended race in the TT calendar, there are (and have been) all kinds of other classes, including even "tiddlers" like a 125cc class. But arguably, a modern 125cc racer is closer to the light, slim pre-war singles of the Senior class than either is to a modern, ultra-fast multi. All racers need to be nimble and sweet-handling, but the light weight of the smaller classes makes them more "flickable." While this may lack spectator appeal on a conventional racetrack, on a course as twisty and demanding as the Island it makes for very spectacular racing.*

nitrous oxide, and experiments with really weird chemicals like nitromethane and hydrazine are commonplace. Every now and then, someone comes up with something new, but usually the new fuels are banned: boranes, for example, offer 25 to 50 per cent more energy per kilo than gasolines, and have a laminar burn rate a hundred times as high as that of gasolines. They are also carcinogenic, and they need very little encouragement to explode or catch fire even when they are sitting in the fuel can.

Turbocharging is normal, and so are multiple engines – often as many as three in a row, in an enormously long frame. Lying full length on a motor that is quite likely to "grenade" (drag racers' argot for "blow up") requires a certain breed of person ....

There are, however, even more bizarre forms of motorcycle sport. For example, there are various types of oval-track speedway racing: on hard surfaces, on cinders, and even (long ago) on wooden tracks. Most of the steering is done by controlling the angle of slide of the rear wheel; the rider's inboard boot is steel-soled to allow foot-dragging and additional steering with the foot. To add to the fun, many American short tracks (typically quarter mile or half mile) have a "jump" built in, to make the motorcycle fly. Riding on any of these short tracks requires very special skills, but the relationship to "real-world" motorcycling is tenuous.

Much the same is true of ice racing, using spiked tyres. No doubt there are people who ride through (say) a Scandinavian winter on spiked-tyre road bikes, but an ice racer is a breed of its own. Again, the races are held on short, oval tracks, usually with spindly-tyred singles. The spikes allow insane angles of lean, with the motorcycle as close as thirty degrees from the horizontal, sixty degrees from the vertical. Riders typically protect their left shins (races are run anticlockwise) with a piece cut from an old, *unspiked* tyre.

And of course there is more. "Sprints" are the English equivalent of drag races, conducted against the clock rather than by comparing two dragsters side by side in an elimination race. There are innumerable classes of speed records. The most obvious variety is absolute speed records for various capacities, supercharged and unsupercharged, and even for specific types of motor (singles, twins, multis) or motorcycle (especially Harley-Davidson), to say nothing of faired and unfaired motorcycles. The 300 mph barrier has long ago been breached, but the "motorcycles" that achieve these speeds look more like rockets or cigar tubes; the last motorcycles to be used substantially unfaired for record attempts were Black Lightning Vincents; as recently as 1955 Russell Wright achieved 185 mph *on a wet public road* on an unsupercharged Lightning. In 1956 a blown 500cc NSU jumped that up to more than 310 mph, while in 1962 a Triumph streamliner hit 224.5 mph. Going back in time, the first speed record is generally regarded as Englishman William Cook's 75.9 mph on an NLG with a JAP V-twin in June 1909. The 100mph barrier fell to Indian in 1920 (104mph), and Joe Wright achieved 150.75 mph on a Zenith-Jap in 1930 – though OEC tried to take

the credit, as it was an OEC that was his main bike; the Zenith was a spare!

Now, of course, there are production motorcycles which are supposed to hit 170 mph out of the box. Even in Germany no one seems habitually to ride that fast, however, for at a comparatively modest 200 kph (124 mph) on the *autobahn*, one is rarely if ever passed by motorcycles – though there is a stream of Porsches, Mercedes-Benzes, BMW motor-cars and occasional exotica like Lamborghini Countaches or assorted Ferraris, all travelling at well over 140 mph (225 kph).

And, regardless of these extremes, and regardless of the law, and regardless of everything else, there are always "dices" on the road, even with the smallest of motorcycles. I can remember thoroughly embarrassing a Kawasaki owner by seeing him off with an East German MZ, a low-powered and weird-looking (and weird-sounding) machine which nevertheless went considerably better round corners than the Japanese machine. Both the MZ and the Kwacker were 250s, his a twin and mine a single, though his must have cost at least fifty per cent more than mine, maybe twice as much. On the straights it was no contest, but as soon as a corner loomed, I had it all. We must both have been in our early twenties. As I said at the beginning of the chapter, racing motorcycles (especially on the public roads) is dangerous and irresponsible. The same could be said about a lot of the other things people do with motorcycles.

But they're fun.

LEFT: *Another Dunlop on the stand: Robert. The majority of spectators want to see the Senior, of course, and even third place elevates a rider to the realm of the demigods. To this day, merely qualifying for a place in the Senior – whether or not you have the faintest hope of winning – remains the ambition of many a road-racer world wide.*

While the dream of riding on the Island exists for riders in all classes, there is more prestige in riding a "full-sized" machine – and not all riders enter state-of-the-art motorcycles. In the 1980s, Vance Breeze (now running Santa Maria Harley-Davidson in California) rode a Harley on the Island. He was not on the winner's rostrum, of course, but how many others under the age of, say, sixty can boast of having raced a Harley-Davidson on the greatest circuit of them all?

ABOVE AND RIGHT: *Steve Hislop hoists the massive trophy high after winning the 1992 Senior. The trophy, a remarkable period piece complete with a winged wheel, is part of a motorcycling tradition which stretches back to the earliest days of racing, and to have one's name engraved on one of the numerous plaques which adorn its base is surely the greatest honour in motorcycle racing ancient or modern. The TT was long ago dropped from the Grand Prix mainstream because some riders thought that it was dangerous. Well, it is; but how dangerous is "too dangerous"? At what point do you call a halt to making GP racing safer? When everyone is riding children's tricycles? They call it "road" racing, after all, and it is disputable whether a race that is not held on a real road is truly a road race. Right, Steve demonstrates a traditional Manx accomplishment: aviating alongside railings. Such skill and concentration is found only in the very greatest road racers.*

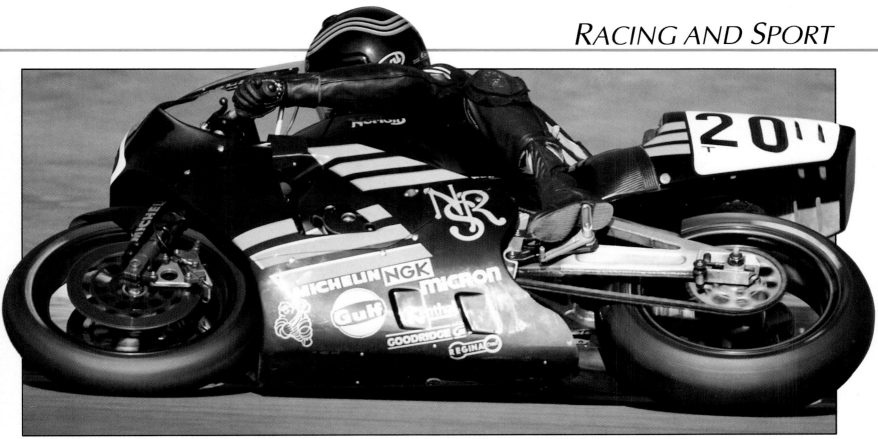

ABOVE AND LEFT: *"Rocket Ron" Haslam can make you forget that Honda, Kawasaki, Suzuki, Yamaha and the rest ever happened. Not only does he ride his Norton with the kind of calm skill that one associates with a bygone age, the motorcycle itself seems to have pursued a separate line of development, both mechanically (Norton is of course famous for rotary engine development) and visually. The elegant black flanks of the Norton still carry sponsors' names, but not in a screaming cacophony of colours and graphics which look as if they were designed by a first-year art student on speed. The same is true of his white-striped black leathers; a magnificent piece of understatement. It was impossible, as the Norton howled past – these pictures were taken in 1991 – not to remember great names from the past, like Geoff Duke: riders who made it look surprisingly easy to ride at average speeds which are higher than many people have ever managed as maximum speeds.*

LEFT: *Don Morley, who shot many of the pictures in this book including this one, is widely regarded as one of the finest motorcycle photographers of all time. Most of us are disappointed when we try to photograph motorcycles, but there are a few basic pieces of "inside knowledge" which can at least make us better. You do not need wildly exotic equipment: a modest SLR camera with a zoom lens of about 80-200mm or 70-210mm is fine for most action shots, while a "standard" 50mm lens is ideal for static shots. You do not need a motor-drive: you will almost always get a better picture by knowing when to press the shutter release and take a single shot than you will by holding the button down and trusting to luck. Even so, you will need to shoot a lot of film: "practice makes perfect" is as true in photographing motorcycles as it is in riding them. Watch everything in the viewfinder, and try to fill the frame with your subject: many shots are spoiled by including material that should not be there, from spectators' heads to ugly backgrounds. Finally, don't be afraid to experiment: for this shot, Don zoomed during the exposure to create this dramatic "burst."*

RIGHT: *A long telephoto lens "stacks up" the motorcycles and makes them appear closer together than they are. The best time to get pictures like this is at the beginning of a race, when the riders are all close together; as the race progresses they will become more and more widely separated, until they are strung out all along the course.*

BELOW: *The beginning of a race, like this 1986 Daytona event, is always the most dangerous time: the field is crowded, and a single spill or stalled engine can lead to a multiple pile-up, so everyone is cautious. On the other hand, riders also need to press on if they are to get out of the "traffic jam" and get ahead. The disarray is clear in this masterful shot.*

RIGHT: *When you meet Kevin Schwanz he seems simultaneously older and younger than you expect. The maturity comes from having ridden faster, in more demanding conditions, than most people can even begin to imagine. The youthfulness comes from the fact that he so obviously enjoys what he is so good at – because you can't get that good at something unless you really enjoy doing it.*

BELOW: *Accidents happen …. At the German Grand Prix at Hockenheim in 1987, Roth and his motorcycle part company in a big way, captured with split-second timing by Don Morley. Suddenly, the functional side of "biker chic" becomes all too obvious, as the leathers and the crash hat are called upon to do the job they are designed for. Why do people take risks like this? Because if you want to race, you have to take risks like this ….*

You learn all sorts of things at a Grand Prix – such as what a Scotsman really wears under his kilt – but the more you learn, the more you can find to puzzle you as well. For instance, everyone knows that tyres have to be warmed up before they exert their maximum grip, but can you really warm up a tyre with an electric blanket, even a custom-made one? You also learn a great deal about national differences as you follow the Grand Prix "circus;" somehow, you would expect to see Pepsi girls at the Japanese GP double-wrapped in two swimsuits, while the single-wrapped young lady just has to be at the Italian Grand Prix.

ABOVE: *Unlike the riders of old, who seemed to be pasted to their machines, modern riders move about in order to get the centre of gravity where they need it. Here, Doohan is half-way out of the saddle as his left knee skims perilously close to the wall. Unfortunately, many "wannabe" racers spend so much time jumping about on their bikes that it actually slows them down.*

LEFT: *Accidents continue to happen …. De Radigues plays a fire extinguisher on his Cagiva in the 1987 Spanish Grand Prix, before it adds insult to injury by bursting into flames as well as throwing him off. As things stand, there is plenty on the bike that can be recycled and rebuilt; if it burns, just about everything is a write-off. What frequently amazes non-motorcyclists is that riders can not only walk away from accidents which look incapacitating; they can also retain the presence of mind to move their machines out of the way, warn other people, and even put out fires.*

LEFT: *More than any other single factor, modern tyre technology has changed the face of motor racing: tyres today are so much "grippier" than they used to be that even machines of thirty and forty years ago can now put up faster lap times than when they were new if they are fitted with current rubber. Here, Kel Caruthers looks at Dunlops, dwarfed by piles of rubber.*

BELOW: *Modern side-car racers look less and less like the outfits of yore, and more and more like three-wheeled Grand Prix cars. The biggest single difference, apart from the missing wheel, is that a Grand Prix car does not have a passenger, much less a passenger who treats the vehicle somewhat as if it were a sailing dinghy. The team here is Webster/ Simmonds.*

RIGHT: *In the dry, slicks give a much better grip, but if there is more than a trace of moisture on the track, more conventional grooved tyres will dissipate it, and grip where slicks will slide. Victory may depend as much on making the right guess about the weather as on the power of the machine and the skill of the rider. This is the Italian Grand Prix.*

BELOW: *A racer like this 1991 Aprilia is a curious mixture of the immaculate and the improvised. The alloy beam chassis and swinging arm are highly polished (which as well as looking good helps crack-detection), but the welds are big and blobby. Then compare the exhaust with the Brembos and the wheels! A very interesting feature is the "upside-down" installation of the Rotax engine, inclined at about thirty degrees downwards from the horizontal; another is the instruments on "outriggers" where the headlamp should be.*

Randy Mamola (above) in repose and (left) in action (hanging off a Cagiva), might not win first prize in a beauty competition; but unlike Hollywood, the Grand Prix circuit will not forgive lack of skill on the track, no matter how many teenage girls' hearts you can set a-flutter. Mamola is good, very good, where it counts: throwing a ridiculously powerful motorcycle around, and making it look easy when it suits him – though he can also pull stunts to make it look difficult, which paradoxically requires more effort than his usual riding style. A rider has to be good to get equal billing with the bike manufacturers and the tyre makers!

An amusing point to notice in the portrait is the "Japlish" on his baseball cap from sponsors Kushitani Leathers: "We are fond of Riders Spirit." But how many of us could do as well in Japanese? For that matter, why is Cagiva's symbol an elephant? The portrait was taken in the 1990 season, and the action shot was at the 1988 Yugoslav Grand Prix.

RIGHT: *in a cloud of smoke, Wayne Davis of Davis Engineering pulls away on his (substantially unsilenced) dragster. The sound is deafening, and the smell takes your breath away. As the smoke clears and your eyes stop watering you realize what an extraordinary sport this is: a man lying on his stomach on a motorcycle which out-accelerates many an aircraft at take-off, and which may (if the engine-builders' calculations are incorrect) "grenade" or blow up in mid-run. And he is so casual that it doesn't even look as if he's wearing any gloves ….*

LEFT: *Vance & Hines are one of the biggest "go-faster" merchants in the United States, and since drag racing is an American obsession, they sponsor dragsters. On this Suzuki-powered bike, you can see most of the distinguishing points of a dragster: the extremely long wheelbase (with the consequent stretched-out riding position), the wheelie bar at the back which prevents the machine from rotating around its own rear axle, and the enormous rear tyre which attempts to transmit several hundred horsepower to the asphalt. The life of the tyres, like the life of the engine, reflects the highly concentrated nature of drag racing: sixty seconds would be a grand prix de l'endurance.*

ABOVE: *In drag racing, the old ways are the best ways. A supercharger saps far more power than a turbocharger, but it delivers the extra boost instantly and with no turbo lag. Messrs Shorrock, purveyors of superchargers to the nobility and gentry for many years, feed twin Norton engines to generate power way beyond the manufacturer's wildest imaginings. Twin and even triple engines are a common way to get extra power, despite obvious objections concerning frictional losses caused by out-of-synch running. Clutches are commonly hydraulic, gearboxes are purpose-built two-speed units, and rigid frames remove many of the problems with rear wheel control which might arise if any real attempt were made at rear suspension.*

143

*Graeme Mitchell pilots a
250cc Aprilia at speeds
which many 500cc road
bikes could not reach.*

PICTURE CREDITS

DON MORLEY: p.1, p.2, p.4, p.6/7, p.8/9, p.10/11, p.12 (top), p.13, p.16/17, p.18/19, p.20/21, p.22/23, p.24/25, p.26/27, p.28/29, p.30/31, p.32/33, p.34/35, p.36/37, p.38/39, p.40/41, p.42/43, p.44/45, p.46/47, p.48/49, p.50/51, p.52/53, p.54/55, p.56/57, p.58/59, p.60/61, p.62/63, p.64/65, p.66/67, p.68/69, p.70/71, p.72/73, p.74/75, p.76/77, p.78/79, p.80, p.82 (bottom), p.86 (bottom), p.87 (top), p.88/89, p.90/91, p.92/93, p.94, p.96 (top), p.97, p.98 (top), p.99, p.100/101, p.102/103, p.104/105, p.106/107, p.108 (top), p.109, 110 (top), p.111 (bottom), p.112, p.114, p.115 (bottom), p.116/117, p.118/119, p.120/121, p.123, p.124/125, p.126/127, p.128/129, p.130/131, p.132/133, p.134/135, p.136/137, p.138/139, p.140/141, p.142/143, p.144. MICHAEL LICHTER: p.14 (top) p.15, p.82 (top), p.83, p.84 (bottom), p.87 (bottom), p.95, p.96 (bottom), p.98 (bottom), p.108 (bottom), p.111 (top), p.113, p.115 (top). GAMMA: p.84 (top). COLOUR LIBRARY BOOKS: p.12 (bottom), p.14 (bottom), p.81, p.85, p.86 (top).